Growing
Perennials

D0117513

Growing Perennials

WRITER
PEGGY HENRY

PHOTOGRAPHER
SAXON HOLT

LAWN & GARDEN

Product Manager: CYNTHIA FOLLAND, NK LAWN & GARDEN CO.

Acquisition, Development and Production Services:
BMR, Corte Madera, CA

Acquisition: JACK JENNINGS, BOB DOLEZAL

Series Concept: BOB DOLEZAL

Project Directors: JANE RYAN, JILL FOX

Developmental Editor: CYNTHIA PUTNAM

Horticulturist: BARBARA STREMPLE

Horticultural Consultant: RG TURNER JR

Photographic Director: SAXON HOLT

Art Director (cover): KARRYLL NASON

Art Director (interior): BRAD GREENE

Cover Design: KAREN EMERSON

Cover Photo: SAXON HOLT

North American Map: RON HILDEBRAND

Photo Assistant: PEGGY HENRY

Copy Editor: BARBARA FERENSTEIN

Proofreader: FRAN TAYLOR

Typography and Page Layout: BARBARA GELFAND

Indexer: SYLVIA COATES

Color Separations: PREPRESS ASSEMBLY INCORPORATED

Printing and Binding: PENDELL PRINTING INC.

Production Management: JANE RYAN, BRAD GREENE

Cover: Combine delphinium, bleeding heart, columbine and sea pink for a lovely perennial flower bed.

First Edition

Library of Congress Cataloging-in-Publication Data:
Henry, Peggy
  Growing perennials / writer, Peggy Henry :
photographer, Saxon Holt.
    p. cm.
  Includes index.
  ISBN 1-880281-12-0
  1. Perennials. 2. Perennials -- United States. I. Title.
SB434.H43 1993
635.9'32 -- dc20   93-20809
                                                        CIP

Special thanks to: Blooms Nursery, Sonoma, California; Valerie Brown; Filoli House and Garden, Woodside, California; Mary Sherwood Holt; Landscapes Unlimited, Petaluma, California; Madrone Manor, Healdsburg, California; Magic Gardens, Berkeley, California; Sandy Maillard; Nancy Miller; Mandi Smith and Curt Morris; Sonoma Mission Gardens, Sonoma, California; Freeland and Sabrina Tanner; Katie Trefethen.

Notice: The information contained in this book is true and complete to the best of our knowledge. All recommendations are made without any guarantees on the part of the authors, NK Lawn & Garden Co. or BMR. Because the means, materials and procedures followed by homeowners are beyond our control, the author and publisher disclaim all liability in connection with the use of this information.

95 96 10 9 8 7 6 5 4 3 2 1

TABLE OF CONTENTS

Why Perennials?

Perennials have been working their magic in gardens for centuries, offering delightfully unforgettable flowers, wonderful fragrances and amazing versatility. And, because they fit into just about any garden setting, blooming year after year, perennials are the perfect choice for new or renewed landscapes.

PERENNIAL CHOICES

It's easy to understand why generations of gardeners have considered perennials essential to well-planned, colorful landscapes. A perennial bed coming to life in the spring offers an irresistible combination of beauty and diversity. Renewability, reliability and almost unlimited potential are just part of the attraction.

Perennials can serve as star players in the garden or as quiet complements to a landscape scene—in a border, along a pathway, in an island bed, in containers—just about anywhere.

With a focus on perennials that are easy to grow, this book explores how to plan, plant and maintain a variety of perennial gardens. Preparing soil, designing a garden, selecting colors, growing from seed and transplanting perennials are all explained. Other information covers dividing, renewing, pruning and propagating perennials to keep them at their best.

Project pages contain how-to information and photos for creating special gardens for cut flowers, for moonlit nights, to attract butterflies and to highlight shady areas. The heirloom garden project focuses on perennials that were grown over a hundred years ago. Also included are instructions for building a window box for a colorful and sweet-smelling perennial display.

Whatever your garden plan, knowing about the plants will help you succeed. The Perennial Gallery (see page 58) offers detailed information of the most beautiful and dependable perennials as well as several perennial grasses. Cultural requirements, climate zones and outstanding features about each plant will help you choose the perennials best suited to the garden you want to create.

Text and photos will guide you in step-by-step fashion through the diverse world of perennials. You may find, once you experience gardening with perennials, that your journey is just beginning.

What Is a Perennial?

A beautiful garden, like the one shown here, often combines many different elements, including annual and biennial flowers, shrubs, trees and perennials. Each plant lends a unique look and charm to the total picture.

Shrubs and Trees All shrubs and trees are assets to the garden since they live longer than three years. Their woody stems do not die to the ground each winter.

Annuals These stock are annuals. They sprout, make flowers, set seed and die in one year.

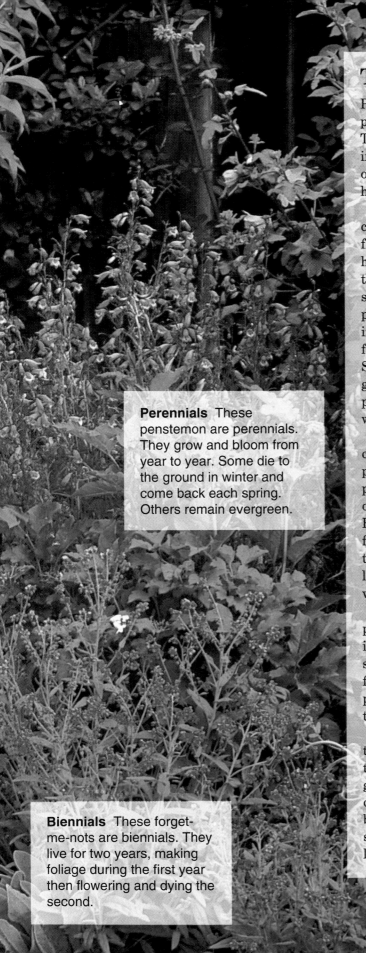

Perennials These penstemon are perennials. They grow and bloom from year to year. Some die to the ground in winter and come back each spring. Others remain evergreen.

Biennials These forget-me-nots are biennials. They live for two years, making foliage during the first year then flowering and dying the second.

TRUE PERENNIALS

Perennials, in simple terms, are defined as plants that live for three years or longer. They differ from trees and landscape shrubs in that they do not have woody stems. Most often, garden perennials are considered herbaceous.

Herbaceous perennials constitute a broad category of garden plants, including many flowering plants and grasses. Most herbaceous perennials die to the ground in the winter with root systems intact, then send out new growth in the spring. Some perennials don't die completely to the ground in cold seasons, but remain as small tufts of foliage that spring up with warm weather. Still others remain evergreen, keeping active, green foliage at all times. Depending on each plant's hardiness or cold tolerance, its growth will vary from one region to another.

Permanence is the key factor in comparing perennials to other flowering plants. Annuals, such as marigolds and petunias, sprout, flower, set seed and die in one year and must be replanted each year. Forget-me-nots and other biennials grow foliage one year, then bloom, set seed and die the following year. Perennials have a longer life cycle. Some perennials live for decades, while others last only a few years.

If permanence and resurgence define perennials, beauty describes them. Nowhere in the plant world will you find more colors, sizes and shapes of flowers. From the round faces of daisies to the deep tubes of foxglove, perennial flowers offer great diversity through every month of the year.

Foliage, texture and form vary greatly too—from tiny-leaved creeping ground covers to silvery mounds to majestic willowy grasses. Choose perennials for a splash of color, a neat and tidy border or a billowy soft backdrop in the garden. They blend well with shrubs, trees and annuals, allowing almost limitless possibilities.

PERENNIAL GARDEN IDEAS

As pleasing as an old friend and as varied as the weather, perennials stand ready for just about any assignment in the garden. Here are a few classic examples to stimulate your imagination as you plan your own spectacular gardens.

Container Garden. For color and warmth on patios, decks, walkways or in entryways, consider perennials in containers.

Perennials in the landscape. Landscaping with perennials offers lots of possibilities. Plant them alone, in groups, or featured as accents in shrub and annual beds.

Cutting Garden. Perennials grow gaily in a cutting garden, providing beautiful bouquets for every room in your house. The plants are grown in rows for easy care.

CAVALCADE OF COLORS

PLANNING COLOR

Many gardeners consider color the most important feature of a perennial garden. To create an effective display, it helps to understand how colors relate to each other.

A color wheel illustrates the relationship of colors. Equidistant around the color wheel are the primary colors of red, blue and yellow. All other colors come from mixtures of these three.

Complementary colors are opposite each other on the wheel—red and green, blue and orange, yellow and violet. Side by side, these colors create a strong contrast.

In between two primary colors, you'll find harmonious colors. These represent a

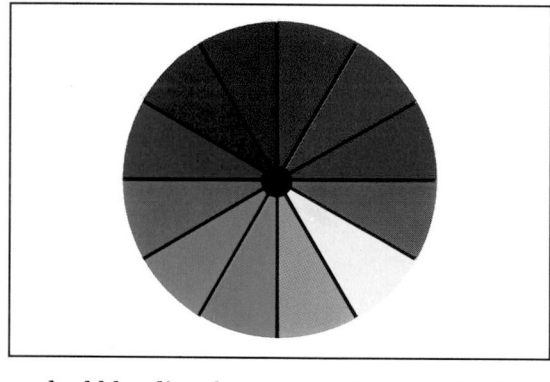

gradual blending from one primary color to the next. For example, starting at blue and moving toward red you see the colors change from blue-violet to violet to red-violet.

Shade, tint and color value describe variations of color. Shades are darker variations of a color and come from adding black. Tints are lighter variations, which come from adding white. Values refer to the brightness of a color—yellow being brighter than blue for example.

This combination of yellow coreopsis, red verbena and blue geranium shows off the three primary colors. These bright colors provide a basis for striking combinations when used with other colors.

Pleasing combinations of pink bee balm and blue veronica show harmonious colors. The closer the colors are on the wheel, the more harmonious they are.

Facing off across the wheel are the complementary colors. Combined in the garden like this blue salvia and yellow achillea, they offer sharp contrasts for visual impact.

Create a warm feel in the garden by combining red, yellow and orange colors, which you find on the right side of the color wheel. These colors enliven the garden.

A restful, refreshing spot in the garden results from combining cool colors—green, blue, violet—from the left side of the color wheel.

Achieve harmonious effects by using different shades of the same color. Light tones combine with darker ones for variation in value or brightness, all of which add interest to the garden.

WORKING WITH COLORS

Striking gardens are usually a result of careful planning. Often, this includes evaluating how colors blend, contrast and stand out individually.

Certain colors seem to go together better than others. Harmonious colors illustrate this: blues harmonize with violets and reds or, traveling the other way on the color wheel, with greens and yellows. The colors work because they are related. Unrelated colors such as pink and orange may seem discordant, although some gardeners appreciate these lively combinations.

Used with discretion, contrast in the garden provides an exciting wake-up call. Where harmonious colors soothe, contrasting colors energize. Yellow and violet flowers contrast; so do the subtler values of cream and lavender. The amount of contrast that is effective in a garden is a matter of personal choice.

An alternative to choosing colors is to plan a one-color scheme. To avoid monotony in this type of garden, vary texture, shape and foliage colors. While any one color can provide rich effects, white is often chosen in a monochromatic, or one-color, garden.

White adds another dimension to the garden when used with other colors. With lighter values, white acts harmoniously. With dark colors, white provides a sharp contrast.

Colors can play tricks with our eyes. Warm colors (yellow, orange and red) seem to jump out, demanding attention; cool colors (blue, green and purple) appear to recede. A clump of bright yellow coreopsis will stand out dramatically next to blue flowers.

For the best examples of effective color use, simply look to nature. Notice the magnificent harmony of fall's burnt orange, gold and burgundy foliage. Remember the visual impact of a red and green-striped caterpillar or a poinsettia.

A Planting Overview

Bringing the Garden to Life

Creating a perennial garden is much like planting other gardens. It takes planning, effort and ongoing attention. At the same time, it can be an exciting and rewarding experience.

The first decision is what kind of garden to create—a quiet sanctuary in the shade, a lively spot with riotous color, an elegant entryway with soft textures or maybe a tiny bed near the patio.

Learn what pleases you. Look through books and visit gardens and nurseries for ideas. Let your imagination take over.

Then study your yard. What sites will accommodate the garden you've imagined? Do you have enough space? Does the location meet the sun, shade and soil requirements for the plants you've selected? If so, great! If not, adapt your idea to fit the space.

Next draw a sketch. It doesn't have to be anything fancy, just a simple plan to tell you what goes where. (Find the basics of garden design on pages 16–17.) It may take several tries before you're satisfied with the design.

The next step is to prepare the bed. Remove weeds, loosen the soil and mix in any amendments the soil needs. After a trip to the nursery, you're ready to set the plants out and begin planting.

You may find the plan changes shape with plants in place. That's not uncommon. Once you see how plants combine you may make adjustments to achieve the look you want.

Your focus will shift to care and maintenance once the garden is planted. Here patience is the key. Once your design comes to life in full color and form you'll know the satisfaction and pleasure perennial gardeners have enjoyed for centuries.

First Decide what kind of garden you want and determine where it will go. Consider exposure to sun or wind, space availability, soil type and maintenance. Stake and measure the area, experimenting with different designs. Use a hose or rope to visualize curves. You may need to try several designs before you end up with exactly the shape you want.

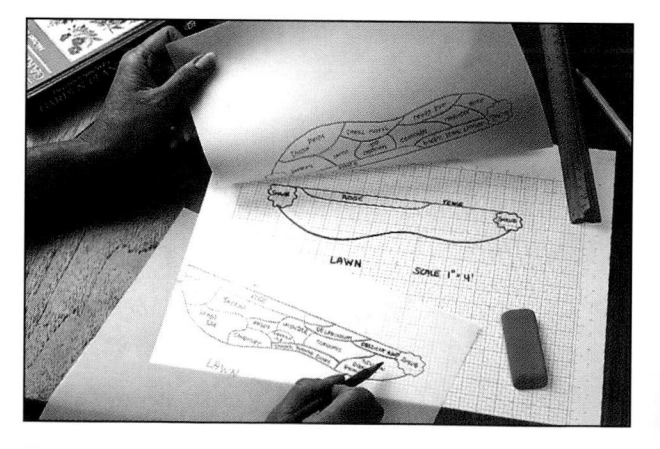

Then Draw a simple sketch of the garden to scale. Use tracing paper to try out various designs on this base plan. Try different combinations of plants in massed groupings or as individual accents. Consider plant height and spread for proper spacing. Draw in any other elements such as pathways, decks, benches or birdbaths.

Third Now comes soil preparation—the foundation of success for your perennial garden. Dig deeply (2 shovel depths), mixing in necessary amendments to create a light, well-drained soil rich in organics such as compost, leaf mold or well-rotted manure. At this time you can mix in dry fertilizer as well.

Next Arrange the plants in the garden according to the plan. You may find that you like arrangements slightly different from what you drew on the plan, depending on how the plants look side by side. As you begin digging your planting holes, tree roots and other obstacles may force you to relocate plants.

Fourth Try growing perennials from seed or buying vigorous plants in 6-packs, 4-in. pots or 1-gal. containers. Avoid plants with roots that have grown in a circle in the pot and large plants that have tangled roots. Double-check selections against your plan to make sure the plants will have adequate space and the proper exposure. To create a garden that matures quickly, choose plants in 1-gal. containers.

Last The perennial garden will grow noticeably in one season, especially if you started with 1-gal. plants. As the plants mature to fill in the spaces, you'll see the overall design taking shape. And when the plants put on that first display of color, you'll feel a definite sense of satisfaction and accomplishment.

PLANNING FOR PERENNIALS

A successful, beautiful perennial garden begins with the plan. Combining the right colors, giving plants correct exposure and spacing and creating interest in texture and form are more easily achieved if you plan ahead. The planning process, with its experimentation and creativity, can be quite rewarding.

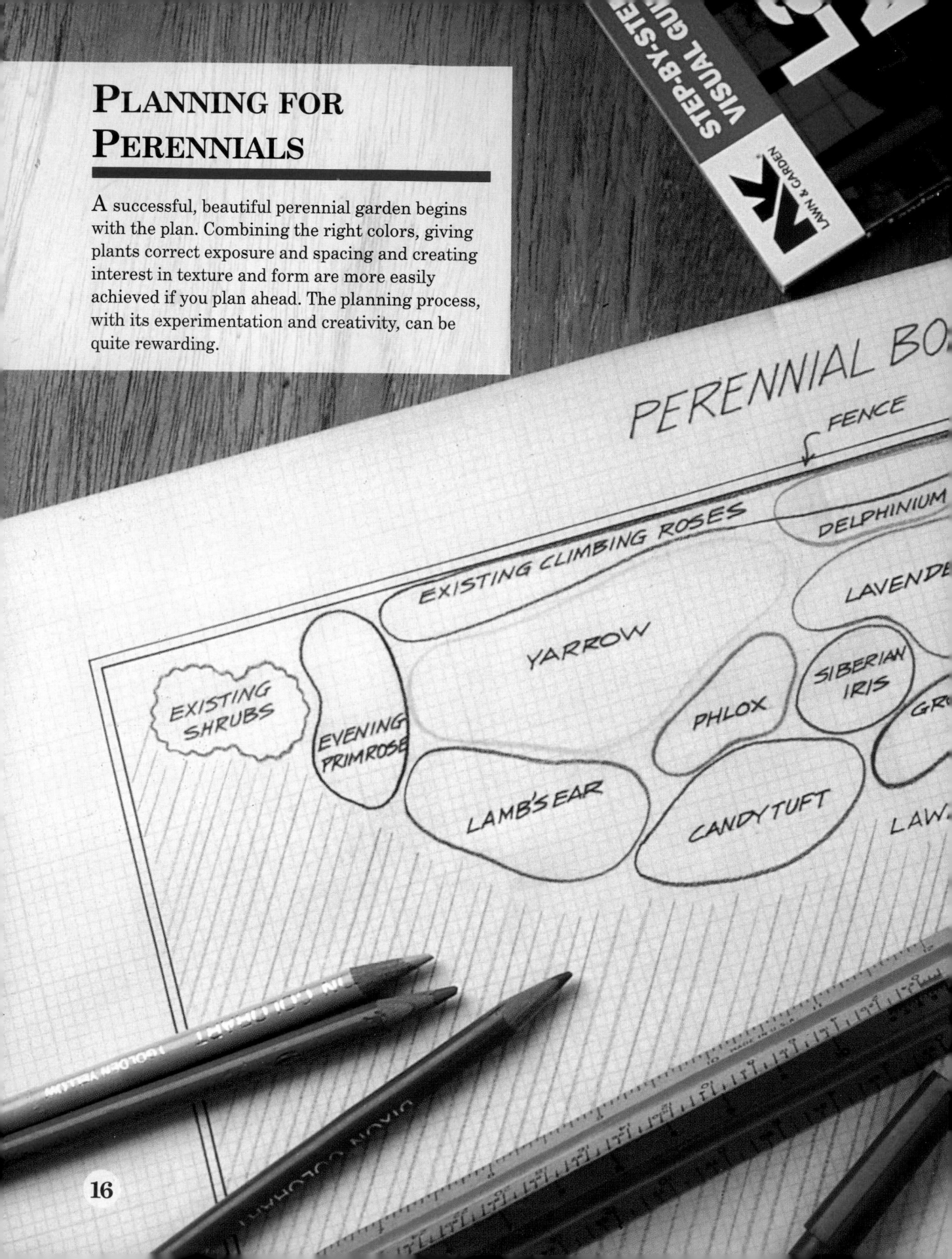

PERENNIAL BO

FENCE

DELPHINIUM

EXISTING CLIMBING ROSES

LAVENDE

YARROW

LAVENDE

SIBERIAN
IRIS

EXISTING
SHRUBS

EVENING
PRIMROSE

PHLOX

GR

LAMB'S EAR

CANDYTUFT

LAW

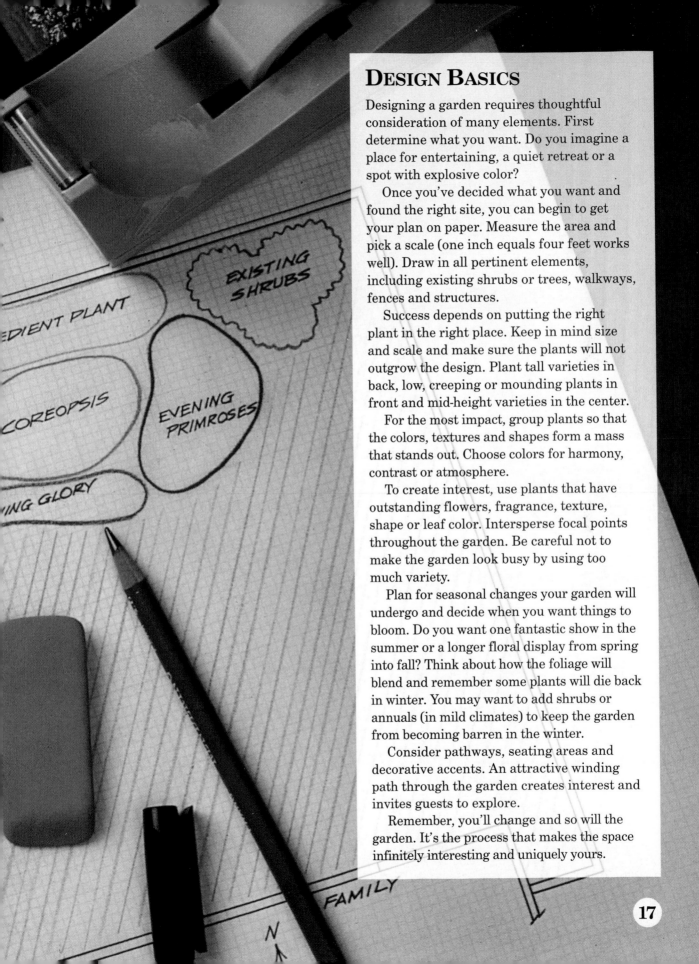

DESIGN BASICS

Designing a garden requires thoughtful consideration of many elements. First determine what you want. Do you imagine a place for entertaining, a quiet retreat or a spot with explosive color?

Once you've decided what you want and found the right site, you can begin to get your plan on paper. Measure the area and pick a scale (one inch equals four feet works well). Draw in all pertinent elements, including existing shrubs or trees, walkways, fences and structures.

Success depends on putting the right plant in the right place. Keep in mind size and scale and make sure the plants will not outgrow the design. Plant tall varieties in back, low, creeping or mounding plants in front and mid-height varieties in the center.

For the most impact, group plants so that the colors, textures and shapes form a mass that stands out. Choose colors for harmony, contrast or atmosphere.

To create interest, use plants that have outstanding flowers, fragrance, texture, shape or leaf color. Intersperse focal points throughout the garden. Be careful not to make the garden look busy by using too much variety.

Plan for seasonal changes your garden will undergo and decide when you want things to bloom. Do you want one fantastic show in the summer or a longer floral display from spring into fall? Think about how the foliage will blend and remember some plants will die back in winter. You may want to add shrubs or annuals (in mild climates) to keep the garden from becoming barren in the winter.

Consider pathways, seating areas and decorative accents. An attractive winding path through the garden creates interest and invites guests to explore.

Remember, you'll change and so will the garden. It's the process that makes the space infinitely interesting and uniquely yours.

BEFORE YOU PLANT

SOIL BASICS

Nothing is more important to the success of your perennial garden than soil. It stores water and nutrients for plant growth and provides a growing medium for roots.

Soil is made up of sand, silt and clay. Alone, these components cannot support much plant life, but together they form a rich, fertile soil called loam.

Sand has the largest particles, which are mainly weathered grains of quartz. It is porous and loose.

Sandy soils are gritty, light and well drained—often too much so. Water penetrates easily and, along with dissolved nutrients, passes right through the sand. Plants in sandy soil need frequent watering and fertilizing. Added to other soils, sand can help improve porosity and drainage.

Silt is a fine, powdery soil made up of very small particles. It is often found deposited near rivers or streams. Silt retains water well but lacks adequate air space.

Clay particles are the smallest of all and pack tightly to form a dense soil. The particles stick together, making it hard for water to penetrate or drain through. Although rich in nutrients, clay soils are sticky when wet and hard when dry, making them difficult to work. Without some type of amendment, clay soils are too dense and poorly drained for most root systems.

Loam is commonly regarded as the best garden soil. A combination of almost equal amounts of sand, silt and clay, it holds nutrients well, has good air space and drains freely. Most soils are actually combinations of the different components—sandy loam, silty clay, silty loam, loamy sand, etc.—and can be improved with the right amendments.

One way to improve the soil and ensure vigorous perennials is to double-dig, loosening the soil to a total depth of 18 in.

IMPROVING THE SOIL

To properly amend your soil, start by evaluating a soil sample or having one tested at a lab. Examine particle size and soil density; then moisten a handful of the soil and look for characteristics of sandy or clay soils. Fortunately, either type of soil can be improved by adding amendments.

Most soil amendments are organic. Organic matter consists of both decaying material from plants and animals and the organisms that break them down. In the soil, organic matter releases nutrients and improves structure. In sandy soils, it fills the tiny spaces between sand particles, absorbing moisture and nutrients. In clay, it wedges between particles to open up the soil for air and water penetration and better root growth.

Compost, peat moss, rotted manure, rice hulls and leaf mold are typical organic amendments that can be used alone or mixed together. Buy them by the bag or in bulk from landscape supply companies. Plan to add plenty of amendment—enough for a four- to six-inch layer.

For the best results, use a fork to dig premoistened soil to a depth of at least 12 inches. Spread the amendments evenly over the loosened surface and mix them in deeply, adding fertilizers with phosphorus and potassium for the root zone (see pages 24–25). Do this in the fall or in spring.

Another effective method of soil preparation is double-digging. Start by removing the top layer (nine inches or so) of soil in a row and setting it aside. With a mattock or spading fork loosen the lower layer another nine inches deep. Then mix in any amendments or fertilizer. Loosen the top layer of the second row and spade the soil into the first trench. Then loosen the lower level of the second trench. Do this all through the bed, filling the last trench with soil set aside from the first. Finally, mix additional amendments into the top layer of soil.

WHERE TO GET PERENNIALS

NURSERY-GROWN PERENNIALS

You can buy time and have a garden that matures quickly if you set out perennials started by a nursery. Most often perennials are available in six-packs, four-inch pots and one-gallon containers.

Six-packs are the most cost effective since you get more plants for your money. But the plants are small and may take longer to mature. Surprisingly, though, the smaller plants will often establish quickly and catch up to plants from larger containers within a matter of months.

One-gallon plants give you much bigger plants to start with and fill in quickly. If they are vigorous, they may nearly fill the garden the first year. Though these cost more, one-gallon plants give you more of an instant garden effect right from the start.

Apart from saving time, nursery-grown perennials have other advantages. Larger plants have good root systems and can generally stand up well to pests and disease. The presence of flowers and foliage helps greatly when you are deciding on plant combinations or color schemes. Larger plants give you an idea of the plant's overall shape at maturity.

For all the good news, starting a garden from nursery-grown plants can have disadvantages. One drawback is choice. Your garden will be limited to those plants available when you plant. Often this means you must either choose those perennials in bloom during the season you start the garden or pick traditional varieties in stock.

Perennials From Seed

Aster
Bellflower
Blanket flower
Chinese lantern
Columbine
Coreopsis
Delphinium
Hollyhock
Oriental poppy
Purple coneflower
Shasta daisy

PERENNIALS FROM SEED

Starting perennials from seed is inexpensive and fairly easy and offers great variety. Purchase fresh seeds suitable for your region. The seed packet lists growing requirements, blooming periods and information on planting.

If you start seeds indoors, sow them in a flat or pot filled with prepackaged soil for germinating seeds. Or use your own mix of half peat moss (or compost) and half perlite, vermiculite or sand. Make sure mix is sterilized to prevent fungus. Do this by "baking" the mix in a 180° oven for two hours.

Light is a key ingredient for sprouted seeds. Fluorescent lights, hung on chains or permanently mounted, work well. Hang lights a couple of inches from the flats. As the seedlings grow, raise the lights six inches or so. For mounted lights, set your containers on inverted pots and lower the containers as the seedlings grow.

It's critical to keep the soil moist so the sprouting seeds and seedlings don't dry out. Thin crowded seedlings so the remaining plants have room to grow.

Transplant seedlings when they have two or three sets of true leaves. True leaves follow the first rounded leaves that emerge at sprouting time. Lift well-developed seedlings—roots, soil and all—from the tray. Never pull a seedling out by the stem; you might tear roots and damage the stem. Repot the seedling in a four-inch pot and water well.

One week before you plant outside, seedlings should be hardened off. Hardening off is a gradual process of introducing the plants to life outdoors. In a spot protected from sun and wind, allow the seedlings a few hours of sun the first day and slowly work up to ten hours by the end of the week. Keep plants watered and cover them at night to protect them from the cold. After the plants adjust to the sun and colder outdoor temperatures, they'll be ready to go into the ground.

TRANSPLANTING
PERENNIALS

Transplanting from Containers

First Set out the plants, making sure they are properly spaced with room to grow. Dig roomy planting holes with plenty of space for the roots to spread.

Next Carefully remove the plant and cut away any roots that are circling. Gently loosen about 1/3 of the roots from the bottom up.

Last Set the plant on a small mound of firm soil. Backfill half way and water to settle the soil. Finish filling, then build a basin around the plant and water again.

INTO THE GROUND

After the seedlings adjust to life outside, they're ready to go into prepared garden beds. To remove the plant, turn the pot upside down, taking care to support the rootball. Tap the pot and slide out the plant along with the soil. Gently set the plant into the planting hole and firm the soil around the roots. Water carefully; after it soaks in, water again.

To pop plants out of six-packs, use your thumb to push up on the bottom of each cell. For four-inch nursery-grown containers, start by tapping the sides of the container. Then turn it upside down and carefully remove the plant. If the plant does not come out easily, give the bottom a sharp hit with your hand. Gently tear off roots that have become matted; loosen others. Set the new plant in the hole so the top of the root zone is at the soil surface. There should be enough room so roots are not cramped.

Plants in one-gallon containers may be older and harder to remove. If they don't slip out upside down after you've tapped the sides, you may need to hit the sides against a rock or hard surface. For stubborn plants slide a knife all the way around the pot edge and rap the pot again.

Once the plant is free, inspect the rootball. Cut off any roots at the bottom that have grown in circles. If the rootball doesn't loosen easily, use a knife to make three or four vertical cuts one-half inch deep around the sides. Then set the plant into a planting hole that is large enough for the roots and deep enough so the plant can sit on a small mound of firm or amended soil in the bottom of the hole and the soil line from when the plant was in the container is even with the top of the hole. Backfill and form a basin around the plant before you water. Water thoroughly.

Weeding is a small job—if you do it regularly. Remove weeds when they are young and have not yet developed seeds or deep root systems.

BASIC CARE

Caring for perennials involves the same basic tasks that go with most gardens—watering, weeding, fertilizing, mulching, protecting against cold and staking. If you keep to a moderate routine, your plants will grow vigorously and reward you with beauty year after year.

Maintaining Perennials

Individual plant requirements and weather conditions will determine how often you water. Soak each plant thoroughly at the base to encourage deep, strong root systems. Water more often but not as long in sandy soils, less often but more deeply if you have clay.

Removing weeds before they form seeds and spread saves work later on. Use a hoe or other tool to get weeds when they're small and easily removed (roots and all).

Fertilizing is an ongoing process. Fertilizers contain three basic nutrients—nitrogen, phosphorus and potassium. Nitrogen (N), listed as the first percentage on fertilizer bags, is essential for lush green growth. Phosphorus (P), listed second, and potassium (K), listed third, are important for overall vigor and flower production. All need to reach the root zone to be effective, so work them several inches into the soil.

Apply fertilizers in granular form when preparing the bed in spring or fall or use liquids after planting. Fertilize before periods of rapid growth and flowering. Slow-release fertilizers release small amounts of nutrients over long periods.

Mulching discourages weeds and cuts down on watering needs. Mulch by spreading several inches of an organic material around the base of the plant a few inches from the stem. Shredded bark or leaves, peat moss, rotted manure or compost work well.

Mulching is also effective for winter protection. Where plants may be damaged by cold, cut all but evergreen perennials to within a few inches of the ground and cover with a six-inch to 12-inch layer of hay, leaves or compost, which you will remove gradually in spring. In very cold areas add up to a foot of mulch.

Staking prevents long flower stalks from falling over. Tie stems loosely to stakes using soft ties. Stakes placed early in the spring will be hidden by the bushy growth later.

CONTROLLING GROWTH

PROLONGING BLOOM

As your perennial flourishes, use pinching, deadheading and cutting back to control growth and prolong bloom.

Pinching is the removal with your fingertips of part of an upward growing stem. This encourages the plant to produce new side shoots, becoming more compact and bushy.

For spring- and summer-blooming perennials, pinch new growth during the growing season to keep plants compact. When pinching to stimulate flower growth of fall bloomers such as chrysanthemums, timing will make a difference. Pinch before July to give new buds time to grow. Pinch just above a bud or leaf. You may need to use shears to pinch a woody stem (called a hard pinch). Chrysanthemums respond well to pinching, as do phlox and sage.

Deadheading–removing spent flowers after they finish blooming–encourages the plant to make more flowers. Many perennials benefit from this, including coreopsis, aster, pinks, pincushion flower and primrose.

Cutting back controls growth by removing material from all over the plant, usually after flowering. Make your cuts above growth buds, as you do with pinching, so growth can be channeled into lower buds.

Also known as heading back, cutting back keeps plants from becoming rangy, can promote a second flowering, removes weak stems and revitalizes older plants. It is also useful for winter protection. Cut back, then cover the plants with a thick layer of mulch. Lavender, candytuft, yarrow, red valerian and artemisia can be cut back successfully.

Perennials that produce single flowers on long stems, such as this coreopsis, are good candidates for deadheading. Often, deadheading results in more flowers. However, in cold climates, deadheading late in the growing season could lead to new growth that may suffer winter damage.

Use pruning shears to cut back perennials, such as this obedient plant, that have a tendency to sprawl. In mild climates, cut back after flowering. In colder climates, cut back perennials after the ground freezes in autumn and cover with a thick layer of mulch.

For compact, bushy plants with more flowers, stimulate side growth by pinching the tips of young chrysanthemums in early summer.

27

DIVIDING PERENNIALS

WHY DIVIDE?

As perennials grow, they form ever-larger clumps of new shoots and root systems. Division gives you new perennials as you separate young plants from the original.

How the perennial grows determines how it should be divided. Divide perennials that form spreading clumps, such as iris, by cutting thick, fleshy underground sections with roots from the main plant. Use a clean, sharp knife for healthy cuts. Ragged cuts open the door to pest and disease invasion. Trim off any broken roots and cut tangled roots by one quarter to stimulate new growth. Cut back the foliage by a third or more to lessen the burden on the new roots.

Some perennials, such as daylilies, asters and hostas, form tight clumps and can be divided by pulling apart the young plants. If the clumps are too thick, separate sections using two garden forks.

For perennials that form small, leafy crowns around the main plant, divide by pulling individual sections apart, again with forks or with your hands. Remove single crowns, roots and all, or separate clumps into larger sections of several crowns each. Divide coralbells, peonies and chrysanthemums this way.

In general, divide spring bloomers after they flower and summer and fall bloomers in early spring. Avoid extremes of heat or cold, since this will stress the new roots. Plants about to bloom should not be divided because they are putting energy into flowers. In colder climates, divide most perennials in the early spring or in late summer after they flower.

Dividing Perennials with Crowns

First Divide in late summer to allow the plant to establish by winter. Soak the plant one day before dividing. Lift out the entire clump.

Third Using your hands, pull off divisions or cut off divisions using a clean, sharp knife. Each division should include at least 3 stems with strong root systems.

Then Use 2 forks, back to back, to pull apart larger sections of the crown. Dispose of any old, weak or diseased sections.

Last Select the most vigorous divisions to replant. Cut the foliage back leaving 5–6 in. Plant the crown at the soil line. Keep the division moist until plants establish.

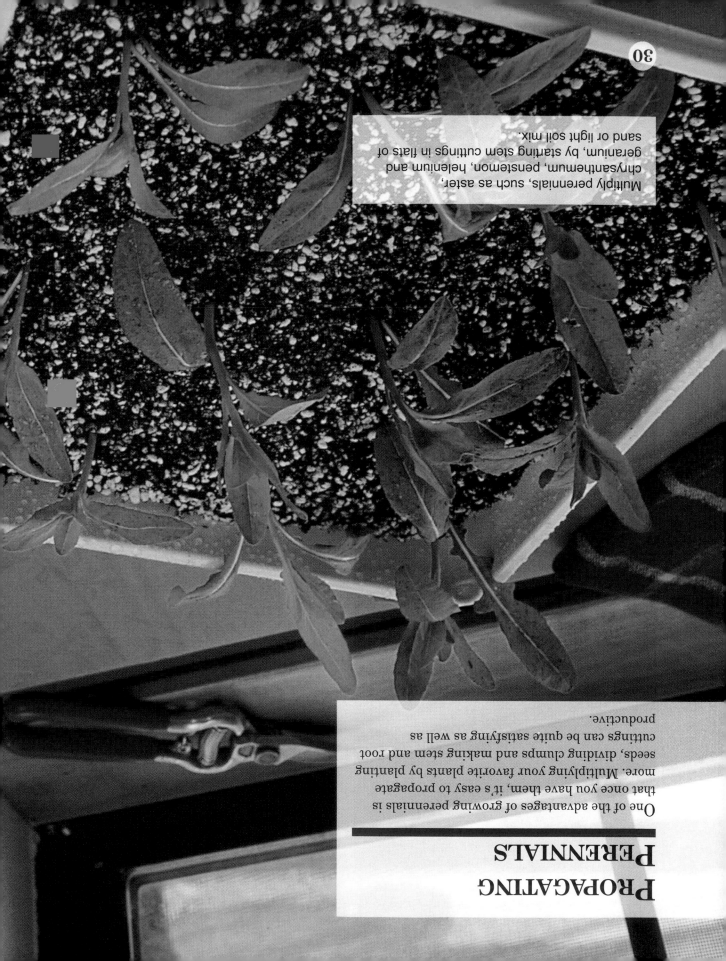

Multiply perennials, such as aster, chrysanthemum, penstemon, helenium and geranium, by starting stem cuttings in flats of sand or light soil mix.

PROPAGATING PERENNIALS

One of the advantages of growing perennials is that once you have them, it's easy to propagate more. Multiplying your favorite plants by planting seeds, dividing clumps and making stem and root cuttings can be quite satisfying as well as productive.

Propagation of Stem Cuttings

Stem cuttings are an easy way to propagate many perennials. During active growing periods cut firm but limber, nonwoody stems with 3–4 leaf joints and no flower buds. Make the cut with a razor blade or sharp knife just below a leaf joint, not in mid-stem. Dip in rooting hormone and insert in a light, sandy soil mix. Water well. If the cutting wilts, enclose the pot in a clear plastic bag, ventilated with a few air holes, to increase humidity.

Propagation of Root Cuttings

Take advantage of an abundance of fleshy roots to make root cuttings. Dig up roots after active growth in mid summer or fall. Separate white, 1/4 in.–thick roots from the rootball and brush off the soil, noting which end was nearer the surface. Cut 3 in. sections with the top end square and the bottom end on diagonal. Cover the root cutting, bottom end down, with a light soil mix and water well.

MULTIPLYING PLANTS

We've looked at starting perennials from seed and by division. Here are two more ways to propagate perennials.

Stem cuttings can be taken during periods of active growth. For spring bloomers, mid summer works well. For those that bloom later, take cuttings in late spring or early summer. Cuttings should be four to six inches long. Cut about one-half inch below a leaf joint, where the rooting will take place. Remove the lowest leaves. To prevent disease and promote good rooting, dip the end in a rooting-hormone powder and shake off the excess.

Next place the cuttings into the growing medium. This should be a sterile (see page 21) mixture of sand, vermiculite, perlite or shredded sphagnum moss. You can also use a combination of light potting soil and equal amounts of the above ingredients.

Gently insert the cuttings two inches deep. Arrange them in rows so their leaves don't quite touch. Water and firm the planting medium and place the container in a bright spot out of direct sun. Keep the soil moist.

In two to four weeks, new growth will appear and plants will resist a gentle tug.

Fall is a good time to try root cuttings. Start with pencil-thick roots and cut them into three-inch sections, making sure each segment has a tiny growth bud or joint.

Cut the top end (nearest the foliage) square and the bottom end on a slant. Place the cuttings in pots or flats of light soil mix containing peat, sand or perlite. Bury the cuttings to a depth of one-half inch. Keep the soil moist. New leaves should appear after several weeks. Oriental poppy, purple coneflower and anemone can be multiplied this way.

Once several good-sized leaves have developed, if you are still four to six weeks from frost, put the cutting in the garden. If you expect cold weather soon, allow the plant to overwinter in a protected spot. Put out the plant after the danger of frost has passed.

DISEASES AND PESTS

METHODS OF CONTROL

At some point, diseases or pests may attack your perennial garden. Your best protection comes from growing strong plants that will be less susceptible to damage and choosing varieties that are resistant to problems in your area.

Keep regular schedules of watering and fertilizing so plants will maintain strong growth. Avoid wetting leaves late in the day, since this can lead to black spot and rust diseases. Remove fallen leaves and flowers where pests often hide and diseases flourish.

Another important consideration is location. For example, it may be that your phlox is suffering from a fungus because it's in a moist, shady spot. Moving it into a sunny, dry spot may end the problem.

Deciding to use controls for diseases and pests is a matter of discretion. Holes in a few leaves and a critter or two will not destroy the garden. When the problem threatens the life of the plants, you may choose to intervene. As an alternative, consider replacing troublesome plants with those that attract fewer problems.

It's safest to choose the least toxic control first, such as hand picking snails or spraying aphids with the hose.

Other environmentally safe controls offer natural-based chemicals that selectively control the damaging insects without harming other insects or wildlife. *Bacillus thuringiensis* is a bacteria that comes as wettable powder. When mixed and sprayed on leaves it becomes toxic to caterpillars, yet it is so safe it can be used on food crops up until harvest.

If you decide you must use an insecticide or a fungicide, do so with care. Read labels thoroughly and follow all recommended procedures.

This leaf has powdery mildew, as indicated by the whitish gray powder. Powdery mildew can attack leaves, stems and flower buds, especially in regions with high humidity. Powdery mildew forms spores that release a fine dust that settles on dry leaves. The leaves become crumpled and distorted. If unchecked, powdery mildew may cause serious leaf loss. Watch for powdery mildew during periods of warm days and cool nights. It might be best to eliminate perennials that are susceptible to this. Should you opt for chemical controls, consider products containing triforine or folpet.

The fungus botrytis has attacked this leaf. Early symptoms are tan or brown spots that progress to a gray mold that can damage leaves and flowers. This stage is quickly followed by rot. Botrytis strikes most often in regions with cool, humid climates. It can hit plants that have suffered frost damage, entering through wounded tissue. To control this fungus remove infected plant parts or use products with mancozeb.

Rust is characterized by small pockets of brown, yellow, orange or red powdery spores on leaf undersides. Upper surfaces of the leaf are mottled with minute yellow spots. Rust can spread through the air or in water; severe cases cause leaf drop. Warm days and cool nights coupled with several hours of moisture invite rust fungus. Begin control by carefully clearing the area around the plant of all fallen leaves and debris. Then remove all infected leaves on the plant. Avoid watering late in the day when leaves cannot dry quickly. Chemical controls include folpet or chlorothalonil and wettable sulfur.

Thrips are tiny—almost microscopic—insects that usually drink plant juices in flowers or buds. New flowers and leaves pucker and open irregularly with twisted, discolored parts that sometimes stick together; leaves may become silvery or tan. Thrips begin to cause problems in late spring and if unchecked become more destructive as the growing season continues. Many natural predators help keep numbers down. Chemical controls for thrips include diazinon and malathion.

Aphids are soft, annoying insects about the size of a pinhead. They can be red, green, pink or black—with or without wings. Aphids prey on new stems by sucking plant juices and sometimes spreading disease. Working in large colonies, they attack leaves or buds. Sometimes the aphids will curl inside the leaf for protection. If natural predators such as ladybird beetles, lacewings, lizards or small birds don't take care of them, try regular hosings with a spray of water. Insecticidal soap is a relatively safe chemical alternative, but for severe infestations you may have to use diazinon or malathion.

Spider mites are tiny speck-like insects that suck plant juices. Evidence of mites is yellowed, lightly flecked leaves that often have fine webbing on the underside. Spider mites do most of their damage during hot weather. Dusty leaf surfaces encourage mites. Natural predators normally keep mites in check. To control mites, hose off leaf surfaces, especially the undersides, for three days in a row. Or spray with an insecticidal soap and water. With either method, repeating the treatment increases effectiveness. Treat severe infestations with light-grade horticultural oil, sulfur or malathion.

COMBINING PERENNIALS WITH ANNUALS

Some things just seem to belong together. Perennials and annuals, for example, team up beautifully to offer spectacular floral displays every season of the year. Perennials, the backbone of the flower garden, lend substance and permanence, while annuals conveniently and quickly add spots of color.

Easy Annuals

Bachelor's button
Coleus
Cosmos
Four o'clock
Impatiens
Marigold
Nasturtium
Pansy
Petunia
Lobelia
Sweet alyssum
Zinnia

A Parade of Color

Perennials are versatile, offering lasting, reliable service in the garden. They bloom faithfully and when the time comes, quietly fade to rest and recharge.

If the goal is to have flowers over many months or flowers filling every space, consider adding annuals (plants that live and die in one year) to the garden. Annuals are easy to grow and inexpensive. They allow you to experiment with color combinations and textures on a temporary basis.

In a young perennial garden annuals can be valuable. They fill in spaces between plants, giving your garden flowers and foliage while you wait for the perennials to come into their own glory. Annuals give the garden a boost of energy and provide a fresh look.

Annuals come in just about every size, shape and color. From five-foot-tall cosmos to low-growing, sweet alyssum, you'll find annuals for any spot among your perennials.

Select annuals as you would any other plant. Pick them according to color, exposure and water requirements, and bloom times. Many annuals bloom in the spring; others shine in summer or fall; and certain kinds even offer winter color in mild climates. You'll probably find that the annuals you plant in one season spill into the next before they begin to decline. You can let them complete the life cycle over a whole year or, if you want constant color, replace plants that have flowered with new ones ready to bloom.

Annuals are available in small and jumbo six-packs, and four-inch pots. Many are easily started from seeds sown indoors or outside.

Annuals don't have the deep root systems permanent plants have, so amending the soil for them isn't as difficult. Annuals require regular fertilizing and watering to sustain them while they bloom. Pinch or deadhead the plants to prolong flower production and keep plants bushy. Remove spent flowers or fallen leaves to keep the garden neat and healthy.

THE MATURING GARDEN

MAKING CHANGES

Any garden is an ongoing project, and a perennial bed or border is no exception. As the garden grows and matures, change is inevitable.

From spring's show of emerging new growth and flowers to summer's colorful display, the garden undergoes rapid change. The process continues into fall when some plants slow while others burst into bloom. Winter ends the show as many perennials take a rest before the process begins again.

Through the years plants expand and mature, sometimes outlasting their usefulness. It may be that a plant simply doesn't perform to your expectations. Maybe the color was wrong or the texture not quite right. Maybe the plant outgrew its space by becoming too large or tall, or maybe it didn't grow enough because of poor conditions.

Whatever your reasons, the time may come to remove a plant. First consider moving the plant to a new location. Experimenting to find the best spot for each plant is part of the process. Fortunately, most perennials survive this. But sometimes the plant simply has to be discarded.

Usually, transplanting takes place at the same time as dividing—during cool spring or, in mild regions, in early fall.

Thoroughly soak the rootball before the move so you can dig it up easily. Then replant to a generous-sized hole where the plant will have room to grow and flourish. Finally, amend and enlarge the old hole to ready it for the newcomer to your perennial garden.

Moving Plants

Transplant during mild weather—in spring or early fall. Soak the plant to be moved. With a shovel or spading fork, loosen the soil about 12 in. out from the center of the plant to determine the extent of the root system. Then, with the shovel dig deeply around the plant at a point that will allow most of the roots to remain intact. You may have to slice through deep or wide-spreading roots or trim others damaged in digging. Carefully lift the rootball out, keeping soil around the roots.

Replacing Plants

Begin the replacement process by loosening the soil at the bottom of the hole; add organic amendments or complete fertilizers as needed and mix in thoroughly. Place a small hill of soil in the bottom of the hole so that the plant will sit slightly above the surrounding soil. Set the new plant in gently and spread out the roots. Backfill halfway and firm with your hands as you go. Water, let the soil settle, then fill with soil to the top. Make a small basin and water again.

WHEN IT'S TIME TO RENEW

MAKING CHANGES

Although, by definition, perennials live three years or longer, most far surpass that, living long and vigorous lives in the garden. But even those given the best of care will eventually reach the end of their life cycle and need to be replaced.

A perennial reaches this stage gradually. You'll notice a decrease in flower production over a few years, and the plant may produce less new foliage. Dark, leafless stems with no active growth may appear at the center of the plant and stems may sprawl. Disease may be a factor in the deterioration of a perennial. Evidence of disease is usually easy to spot. You may find discolored or distorted leaves, stunted growth, weak stems, overall wilt or damage by pests. Sometimes weather extremes such as prolonged drought or unexpected freezes cause plants to decline.

If the disease or damage is so severe that it requires chemical controls, or if the plant has passed its prime, removing the plant makes sense.

In some cases, you'll decide to replace a plant because it has become overgrown. A plant struggling in a space too small for it will not grow well and could crowd neighboring plants.

Depending on how overgrown the plant has become, you may need to cut it back to make it easier to handle before you take it out. If it is healthy, find a spot where it has room to grow and transplant it with care (see pages 36–37).

Renewing a Perennial Bed

Remove perennials that have died out in the middle and become weak and rangy. Dig completely around the rootball, removing as many roots as you can.

For perennials with disease or other damage, cut back all foliage, stems and flowers and dig up root systems.

Overgrown plants can crowd neighboring plants, block light and detract from the garden design. Trim the plant prior to moving it to a better location.

BUILDING A WINDOW BOX

CREATING A VIEW

Window boxes are ideal for creating miniature perennial gardens with unique charm. Many plants do well in such confinement, trailing over the edges or sending sweet scents through open windows. In all but mild climates, protect plants during winter.

Building the box is not difficult but should be undertaken with care. Use sturdy one inch–thick wood suitable for outdoors and secure the sides with two-inch galvanized wood screws and L brackets. To attach the box to the house, use five-inch rust-proof metal brackets that can support the combined weight of box, moist soil and plants.

Be sure the box is not situated directly above paths or walkways, or positioned where it might become overloaded with snow. Avoid placing the box where it will interfere with the operation of the window. Remember, too, water draining from the box falls on anything directly below.

Choose perennial varieties that do well in limited space and stay fairly small and bushy. Trailing and fragrant perennials work beautifully. Primroses of all kinds, violas, pinks, trailing geraniums, candytuft, forget-me-nots, small salvias, dwarf asters, snow-in-summer, catmints and dwarf chrysanthemums are just a few good choices.

Maintaining the window-box garden is much like maintaining any container garden. The plants, especially those in sunny spots, will require frequent watering. Fertilize regularly and groom as necessary.

Assembling the Box

First Take exact measurements of the window. Pick a style for your box and determine its width, height and depth. The deeper the box, the more room the roots will have.

Then Make a materials list. You'll need 1 in.–thick lumber for sides and bottom, galvanized screws and nails, L brackets and brackets for hanging. Use lumber suited for outdoors such as redwood or cedar.

Third Construct the box by joining front and back to sides using 2 in. nails or wood screws. Attach the bottom section along all sides.

Fourth Drill several 1/2 in. drain holes around the perimeter and in the center of the bottom. If you did not use rot-resistant wood, line the bottom with ventilated plastic. Paint as necessary.

Fifth Affix and level 5 in. or larger metal brackets to wood or masonry siding. Brace underneath with L brackets or wooden shelf supports for extra security.

Sixth Set the box on brackets and double-check that it is level. Use 1 1/2 or 2 in. wood screws to attach brackets to box. Insert screws carefully so they do not protrude through sides.

Seventh Fill box with commercial potting mix or with one part each loam, sand, perlite and peat moss. Mix in water-holding polymer crystals (use half indoor rates) and slow-release fertilizer.

Eighth Select healthy plants. Look for perennials that stay compact, offer fragrance or have trailing habits. This window box contains dianthus, ivy geranium, campanula and viola.

Last Remove the plants from containers and loosen the roots. Set the plants an inch or so below the rim. Firm the soil. Water well and add soil to low spots.

PERENNIALS IN CONTAINERS

Besides being versatile in the garden, perennials are also wonderful plants for containers. Place containers on the patio, near the front door or just outside the dining room window, to enjoy a continuous, colorful display from perennials.

Perennials for Containers

Alstroemeria	Gazania
Beard-tongue	Geranium
Bellflower	Ivy geranium
Candytuft	Lilyturf
Cinquefoil	Pincushion flower
Coreopsis	Primrose
Chrysanthemum	Salvia
Daylily	Sea lavender
Dianthus	Stonecrop
Evening primrose	Verbena
Fleabane	Sweet violet
Gaillardia	Yarrow

A GARDEN UP CLOSE

A perennial container garden gives you a portable, small-space alternative to larger beds. Perhaps your patio or deck needs a splash of color or maybe you want to tuck in something around the base of a tree. For a striking look, cluster several containers together.

Another advantage with containers is almost year-round color. Replace plants that have flowered in spring with summer- then fall-blooming perennials. For lasting effects select varieties that have long bloom times. Plant individual perennials or mix several kinds for a bouquet. Fill in with annuals.

An abundance of containers makes it easy to fit all tastes and price ranges. Ceramic and terra cotta pots are beautiful but can be heavy and dry out fast. Plastic pots hold moisture and are inexpensive and light. Wood containers are attractive, but may not last long unless made from rot-resistant wood.

The best perennials for containers tend to be those with compact or trailing growth habits. Taller, larger plants look out of proportion in containers and usually need more space too.

Soil is the most important factor in a successful container garden. The growing medium needs to be light and fast draining yet moisture retentive. Commercial potting mixes work, or you can use the same mixture recommended for the window box (see page 41). By mixing in slow-release fertilizer granules when you plant, you'll avoid fertilizing chores during the growing season.

The container garden will require more water and fertilizer than plants in the ground. If you mix polymer crystals into the soil, you'll need to water less because the particles absorb hundreds of times their weight in water.

Remove spent flowers and groom container plants regularly to keep them looking their best. In cold regions when winter plants go dormant, cut them back to a few inches, cover with mulch and move them to protected areas.

HEIRLOOM PERENNIALS

Perennials are survivors—plants that hold on in winter to grow back in spring, just as they've done for hundreds of years. Today we can enjoy old-fashioned heirloom perennials very much like those George Washington planted at Mt. Vernon or that early settlers admired in their gardens in the 1800s.

Heirloom Garden
A = carnation; **B** = lamb's-ears; **C** = foxglove; **D** = daylily;
E = Stokes' aster; **F** = sweet violet; **G** = candytuft;
H = dianthus; **I** = yarrow; **J** = columbine

OLD FAVORITES

Heirloom plants are generally considered to be those introduced to American gardens from 1600 to about 1950. This includes native herbs, flowers, shrubs, vines and trees as well as plants from around the world. Antique or ancient types sometimes date back to classical times, while the middle-aged plants appeared toward the end of the nineteenth century. Into the latter category come many perennials grown in old English cottage gardens and early American gardens from Maine to California. Their easy-to-grow, tolerant and tough nature still makes these perennials prime candidates for your garden.

It's amusing to imagine, as you plant an airy yarrow or a sunny daylily, that George Washington kneeled in his knickers at Mt. Vernon planting nearly an identical plant. It's also incredible to think that even though the world has changed dramatically, the perennials in an heirloom garden grow and flourish today just as they did over 200 years ago.

Design the heirloom garden using the same principles you would use for any perennial garden (see pages 16–17). Consider your color scheme (see pages 12–13) and plant combinations with both flowers and foliage in mind.

Plant a bed of only heirloom perennials, as we've done here. Or mix in trees, shrubs, vines, bulbs and other plants. There may be slight differences between heirloom and today's plants, but overall the garden s should be close to those from centuries ago.

In this garden we feature carnation, evergreen candytuft, Stokes' aster, sweet violet and woolly lamb's-ears—all of which George Washington grew at Mount Vernon. The pink yarrow is a North American native; columbine and daylily were typical choices in early settlers' gardens in the 1600s.

Many of the perennials featured in the gallery at the back of the book are also heirloom or old-fashioned selections.

PERENNIALS ON THE ROCKS

Rock gardens combine grace and beauty with strength and tenacity. A rock garden, with its tiny plants, can be a delightful option to a larger perennial bed, an intriguing collection of unusual plants or a small mounded garden that becomes the focal point of your backyard.

Rock Garden
A = sea thrift; B = dianthus; C = bellflower; D = alpine aster; E = coralbells; F = iris

MINIATURE MARVELS

Not everybody has a spacious yard with dark, rich loamy soil perfect for a robust perennial garden. Fortunately, rock gardens flourish without these luxuries.

Rock gardens are not only pleasing to the eye—they're functional too, thriving where other plantings would fail. They're great in sloping areas and spots with rocky soil, but you can create a rock garden just about anywhere by adding mounds and boulders.

To obtain a natural look include small plants that spread over the rocks or form mounds of foliage and flowers.

In this garden we've used artemesia, bellflower, pinks, coralbells, creeping phlox, sea thrift, iris, stonecrop and candytuft. Many more would fill the bill just as well; you'll find notations of these in the perennial gallery beginning on page 58.

You may want to include permanent shrubs or small trees in your rock garden. Japanese maples, small pines and dwarf fir trees blend well with perennials. Azaleas, daphne, heather, dwarf barberry and juniper are only a few of the many shrubs suited to rock gardens.

As you design your rock garden, remember to imitate nature. If adding rocks, bury them so they look natural. Keep proportions small and selections simple. In nature you rarely see scores of different plants within a small space. More often, you find drifts of a few plants with occasional individuals serving as focal points.

Rock garden plants share common requirements. Most like sun and moderate water and all need a well-drained soil. If your soil doesn't provide adequate drainage, mix in plenty of organic material (see pages 18–19), or construct mounds using amended soil.

Maintenance in the rock garden is key. Remove weeds before they get big. Water when plants are young or begin to wilt. Fertilize lightly before active growth or flowering periods.

GROWING IN SHADE

Who can resist the cool sanctuary of a shade garden on a hot summer day? That's what you will enjoy, along with glorious flowers blending to perfection, in a perennial shade garden. Such a garden is special for the atmosphere it creates and the plants it features.

Shade Garden
A = plantain lily; **B** = bleeding-heart; **C** = bergenia; **D** = columbine; **E** = astilbe; **F** = astilbe; **G** = lilyturf

A COOL RETREAT

Many perennials thrive in shady spots—under the canopy of a tree, along the north or east side of the house or under an arbor.

Start by tracking the sun from morning through late afternoon to see how much sunlight reaches the garden. Remember that the sun changes its angle in the sky through the seasons, and that after they lose their leaves in winter, deciduous trees will let more light in.

Full shade is found under a thick tree canopy where no sun penetrates. Partial shade is found under an open tree canopy where filtered sunlight reaches the ground, or on the north side of a building where only early morning or late afternoon sun strikes.

The kind of light the garden gets is important. Dappled, indirect or early morning sunlight won't harm perennials needing protection or plants that like some sun. But direct, hot sun even for a few hours in the afternoon could be deadly for shade-lovers. Watch for reflected light and heat in front of brick, stone or house walls.

Plan for irrigation, since shade plants typically are moisture-lovers. Small gardens might be watered by hand, but larger areas will be easier to maintain if you have a drip or underground irrigation system.

Since a shade garden invites exploration and offers retreat, you may want to plan for seating areas, patios and decks. Water features such as birdbaths or fountains add to the refreshing atmosphere.

Perennials for shady spots generally combine well and offer beautiful flowers and foliage. Remember that when plants go dormant, the garden will not have the lush, enticing look it had in summer. Consider including evergreen shrubs, annuals or bulbs (in mild climates) for form and substance during winter.

Here we combined astilbe, hosta, columbine, creeping lilyturf and bleeding-heart. Look for other shade-loving perennials in the gallery.

ATTRACTING BUTTERFLIES

Butterflies are delightful garden visitors, dancing among the flowers with carefree grace. With the right kinds of plants you can create a striking informal garden that attracts these marvelous guests.

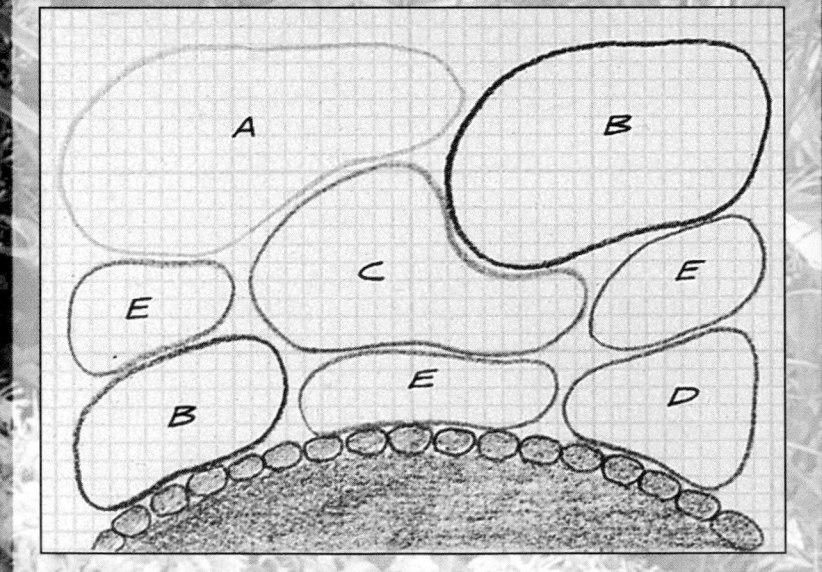

Butterfly Garden
A = coneflower; **B** = purple coneflower; **C** = gay-feather;
D = bee balm; **E** = butterfly weed

ENTERTAINING GUESTS

Gardens offer unique opportunities for observing nature. Many of the plants we enjoy in the garden provide vital food or shelter for butterflies, birds and other creatures.

You can plan a specific garden to attract butterflies or plant the perennial garden near a natural area where grasses and other plants already provide food and shelter for caterpillars and their cocoons. As a bonus, your garden may attract hummingbirds and songbirds.

Caterpillars will most likely be present in the butterfly garden as well. If you can tolerate a few chewed leaves and avoid using pesticides, the butterflies should more than compensate for a bit of untidiness.

In general butterflies are attracted to fragrant flowers with single rings of petals and large centers from which they can easily drink the nectar. They tend to favor white or brightly colored flowers, often with dark centers; flowers or flower clusters must be large enough for the butterflies to land on.

As you design your garden keep in mind the rules we've been using—plant in masses, place tall plants in back, keep things in proportion and consider maintenance. A butterfly garden grown without pesticides or herbicides will require regular weeding and watering and occasional fertilizing.

In this garden we used purple coneflower, bee balm and gay-feather. Other choices include butterfly weed, lavender, phlox, coreopsis, delphinium, sea thrift, pinks, candytuft, primrose, Michaelmas daisy, stonecrop, red valerian, black-eyed Susan and chrysanthemum.

As with some other gardens, it may be useful to consider adding annuals, bulbs, shrubs and trees to fill in the garden in winter.

Butterflies are attracted to such annuals as sweet alyssum, petunia, ageratum, stock, zinnia and cosmos. The number one shrub to include is the butterfly bush, *Buddleia* sp., which is guaranteed to attract butterflies as it blooms through spring and summer.

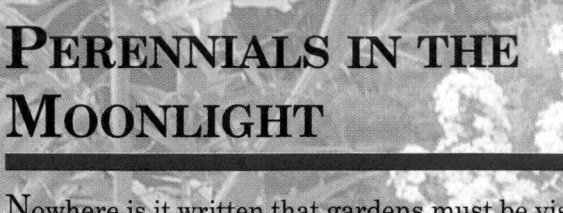

Perennials in the Moonlight

Nowhere is it written that gardens must be visited and enjoyed only by day. Although hundreds of perennial flowers shine under the sun, certain plants save their splendor for soft moonlit nights. These special flowers bounce moonbeams off their petals or send out sweet scents after dark.

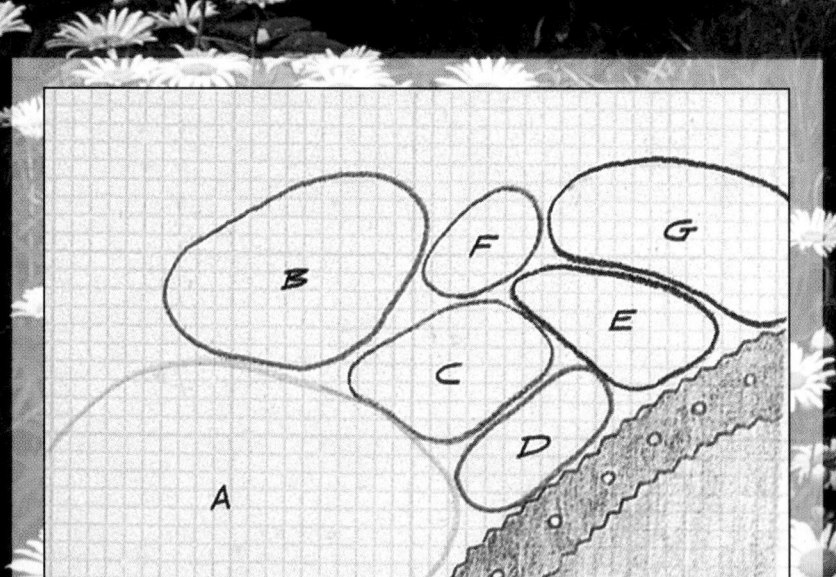

Moonlight Garden
A = shasta daisy; **B** = phlox; **C** = yarrow; **D** = lamb's ears;
E = dianthus; **F** = orris root iris; **G** = yarrow

EVENING STARS

Some gardens seem to come alive at night. Certain flowers capture the moonlight while others wait until the cool of the evening to release their fragrances. Those with silvery foliage hold the light and almost glow.

Locate the garden where it will be visible at night. Plants featured near a walk, clustered around a seating area or planted just off a patio should have dramatic nighttime effects for garden visitors. Avoid areas where street or home security lights might interfere. Keep in mind how the garden will look in daylight.

Instead of a complete garden, you may choose to use individual plants at various places in the perennial garden or in a mixed border. They will serve beautifully as focal points on bright nights and the garden will have overall appeal in daytime as well.

Create a movable moonlight garden by planting in containers. Place the plants on a moonlit patio or cluster them on a deck or balcony where they will catch the light. When there's no light from above, move the containers to any convenient spot.

Several perennials have pale flowers perfect for moonlit gardens. Choose from yellow and pink daylilies (some varieties stay open at night, others do not), evening primrose, shasta daisy, candytuft, beard-tongue, primrose or geranium.

Other perennials will release nighttime fragrances. Seen in this photograph, orris root iris, *Iris pallida* 'dalmatica', has fragrant flowers and striking leaves. Madonna lilies, actually perennial bulbs, display their fragrant pure white June flowers on three- to four-foot stems. Carnations, phlox and clove pinks also provide a wonderful sweet scent for the moonlight garden.

Silvery foliage in the moonlight makes a bold statement. Try artemisia, yarrow, lavender or woolly lamb's-ears. The gray leaves also add interest during the day because they combine so well with green foliage.

53

CUT FLOWERS

BRING THE BEAUTY INDOORS

Many perennials make perfect cut flowers for you to enjoy indoors or share with friends. You can grow the cutting garden with plants set out in rows for easy harvesting. Or simply add perennials for cutting to beds and borders in the landscape.

Good choices for the perennial cutting garden are gay-feather, pincushion flower, purple coneflower, chrysanthemum, salvia, dianthus, bleeding-heart, delphinium, perennial sunflower, peony, bee balm and the obedient plant.

A successful cutting garden starts with thorough ground preparation. Add plenty of organic amendment if your soil is heavy with clay or overly sandy. Mix in a complete or slow-release fertilizer.

Give the plants plenty of water. Apply liquid fertilizer just prior to and during active growth. Keep weeds and pests in check.

Cutting flowers frequently require staking. Many of the plants have slender stems that cannot support heavy flowers. To keep the flowers looking their best, stake before stems become top heavy. You can use broken sticks, brush or bamboo stakes. Single green metal stakes or links of several stakes virtually disappear into the foliage. Use soft ties of felt or twine or plastic green garden tape to attach stems to stakes.

Harvest time comes at the peak of bloom. Cut the flowers as buds begin to open, but before they are fully unfurled. Cut them when their water content is high—early in the day or during the early evening. Don't take wilted flowers. Using sharp shears, cut above a leaf or growth bud and quickly immerse the stems in water. Recut the base of the stems underwater.

How to Cut Flowers

First Cut the stem using an underwater cutting device. Or immerse the stem in a bucket and recut. This keeps bubbles of air from blocking the stem and preventing the intake of water.

Next Plants with milky sap are best preserved by searing the ends. Use a flame or dip 1/2 in. of the stem in boiling water to seal in important fluids.

Last Dissolve floral preservative in a vase filled with tepid water. The preservative gives the flowers nutrients. Display the arrangement in a cool spot and check daily to make sure the water level remains high.

Cut Flowers

Aster	Dianthus
Astilbe	Gay-feather
Baby's breath	Gloriosa daisy
Bee balm	Lavender
Black-eyed Susan	Obedient plant
Blanketflower	Oriental poppy
Bleeding-heart	Pincushion flower
Carnation	Purple coneflower
Christmas rose	Salvia
Chrysanthemum	Scabiosa
Coreopsis	Veronica
Delphinium	Yarrow

DRYING PERENNIALS

You can extend the enjoyment of your perennials by drying the flowers for everlasting bouquets. Drying holds the flower color and form beautifully for arrangements or wreaths. Easy methods for drying include hanging or using silica gel crystals.

First Cut flowers at the peak of bloom early in the day. Remove the flower and stem with sharp shears. Strip away leaves and gently shake off excess moisture. Good perennials for drying include peony, delphinium, yarrow, salvia, Christmas rose, carnation, gloriosa daisy, baby's-breath, feverfew, hollyhock and phlox.

Or To dry using a silica gel, surround and cover single flowers in air-tight containers of silica gel crystals. The sand-like particles absorb moisture and can be reused if heated in the oven. This method is great for preserving color and form of individual florets of delphinium, for Christmas rose, gloriosa daisy, hollyhock, feverfew, phlox and peony. Check flowers after a week. If the petals are crisp, the drying is complete; use this test for all drying methods.

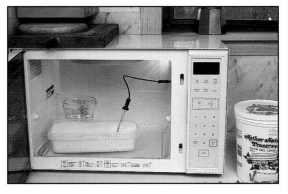

Next To hang-dry, bundle flower stalks loosely and hang—heads down—in a dry, dark warm place such as an attic or a closet. Hang several bunches from a wire coat hanger to save space. Try baby's-breath, salvia, chrysanthemum, statice and yarrow using this method.

Last Microwaving flowers prepared in silica gel speeds the drying process but does not replace it. Use a microwaveable container. Insert microwave thermometer in gel and put a cup of water in the corner of the oven. Microwave for 30–60 seconds or until thermometer reads 220° F. Remove, cool and finish drying flowers at room temperature as in previous method.

PERENNIAL GALLERY

SO MANY TO CHOOSE

There are so many wonderful perennials—hundreds in fact—that it was difficult to select those to highlight here. Many cultivars and old-time favorites that were excluded are just as valuable and versatile as the perennials that are featured. The focus of this gallery is on dependable, easy-to-grow plants that will adapt to many areas.

The plants are listed by common name. Each plant is also identified by its scientific name: genus, species and, in some cases, variety or cultivar. Since common names can vary, scientific names provide a more accurate way to identify plants.

The gallery entries cover flower color and form, plant size and shape, growing tips, special uses and hardiness zones based on the United States Department of Agriculture's minimum temperature map. (You'll find that map on pages 76–77.)

This gallery is designed to give you an introduction to a few of the many perennials available to you. You may find differences in how plants perform depending on soil type and soil preparation, variations in climate and other growing conditions. Zones are listed for all plants within a genus or group. Occasionally, individual perennials within the group may not be as hardy, so always check with your local nursery or garden center for specifics about plants available in your area.

In some gallery entries individual plants are featured, such as the blanket flower, *Gaillardia grandiflora*. In other cases, where several perennials within a plant group deserve consideration, we talk about the genus as a group of species, such as with various bellflowers, or *Campanula* species. In almost all cases, more plants per grouping are available than we could cover.

Alstroemeria
Alstroemeria species and hybrids

The striking Alstroemeria or Peruvian lily is characterized by loose clusters of streaked or speckled 4 in. flowers. Plants grow in clumps reaching 1–5 ft. Foliage is lily-like and flowers come in pink, orange, yellow, red, lilac, white, cream and orange—some accented with dark markings. Use in massed color in late spring to mid summer, for cutting or in containers. In areas of frost, dig up the tender, brittle tuberous roots carefully, divide any matted clumps and store over winter. Or plant 6–8 in. deep and mulch in winter. Give ample water in well-drained, highly organic soil. Likes sun except in hot summer regions. Zones 7–10.

Aster
Aster species

Showers of late summer and autumn flowers bloom on perennial asters that range in height 6 in.–6 ft. The Michaelmas daisies, known botanically as *A. novae-angliae* and *A. novi-belgii,* have delighted gardeners for generations. Hundreds of plants fall into this broad category. Give them lots of sun, a well-drained soil and regular watering. Watch for powdery mildew, stake tall varieties, pinch for compact growth and divide vigorous growers every 2 years. Asters are useful in borders and in rock and cutting gardens. *A. frikartii* is an excellent 2 ft. choice, blooming all summer. Zones 4–9.

Avens

Geum species

Avens have bright flowers in red, orange, yellow, bronze and other warm colors. They form clumps 6 in.–2 ft. high with single or double rose-like flowers from spring through early summer. Some have dark green, toothed leaves; others offer clumps of hairy foliage. The tallest and arguably showiest is *G. quellyon* with slender stems supporting flower clusters 2 ft. above the foliage. Geums prefer full sun, well-drained, humus-rich soil and regular watering. Plant them 12 in. apart and divide in the spring as plants become crowded. Zones 4–10.

Beard-tongue

Penstemon species

Tall spires of tubular flowers mark these easy perennials that thrive in the sun. Blooming in spring and summer, plants reach 2–4 ft. with slender stems and flowers in white, pink, red, blue and purple. Many have showy white throats or attractive spotted inner petals. These drought-tolerant perennials are short-lived, lasting only about 4 years, but their prolific flowering periods make them valuable additions to perennial beds. New plants are easily started from cuttings. Give penstemon full sun, average water and a light, well-drained soil. Soggy soil will prove fatal. Cut back after spring or summer flowering and you'll get a repeat bloom. Zones 5–10.

Baby's-breath

Gypsophila species

Baby's-breath perennials are light and airy with many branches, few leaves and tiny flowers. The grayish foliage seems to disappear amid the delicate flowers that are perfect for cutting and drying. Plants range 1–4 ft. and summer flowers come in white and pale and dark pink. 'Bristol Fairy' has double white flowers and reaches 3 ft. 'Perfecta' offers larger white flowers. *G. repens* is a trailing rock-garden specimen. Plant them all in full sun in a well-drained, alkaline soil. Add lime to acid soils. Support plants to keep them from flopping over. Grow from seed or cuttings. Zones 3–10.

Bee Balm

Monarda didyma

This favorite of American settlers in the 1700s is a member of the mint family, and its aromatic leaves make a refreshing tea. The plant produces ragged clusters of tubular flowers on 2–4 ft. stems in summer. Colors include violet, pink, red, white and mahogany. Foliage forms dense spreading clumps of lance-shaped leaves. Plants prefer sun to part shade, moist, organic-rich soil and regular to heavy watering. Divide every 3–4 years in the spring. Use in masses, to attract hummingbirds and in areas where it can sprawl. Zones 4–9.

PERENNIAL GALLERY

Astilbe

Astilbe x arendsii

Plumes of feathery flowers rise above fern-like foliage on these early-summer blooming perennials. Stalks range 1–5 ft. Astilbe, also known as false spirea or meadow sweet, stays nicely mounded, offering flowers in red, pink, rose and white. Some boast attractive bronze leaves; all have a clean, slightly glossy look. Astilbes like moist, but not soggy soil, rich in organic matter. Plant in fall or spring in sun—or part shade in regions where summers are hot. Dwarf astilbe, *A. chinensis* 'Pumila', has a creeping habit that is attractive as a ground cover. Use astilbe in masses, shade gardens, near pools and ponds and along border fronts. Zones 4–10.

Bellflower

Campanula species

There are over 200 species of bellflower, so named because their blue, lavender, white or purple flowers form bells or cups of various sizes. Bellflowers range 8 in.–5 ft. tall on small spreading or upright clumps. Bellflowers bloom in spring and summer and have long been popular choices for cottage gardens. Serbian bellflower, *C. poscharskyana*, is a wonderful little ground cover with heart-shaped leaves and starry blue flowers perfect for a rock garden. *C. lactiflora* is a tall variety that is easy to grow. Give bellflowers sun or partial shade, regular watering and average, well-drained soil. Zones 3–10.

Black-eyed Susan

Rudbeckia species

Black-eyed Susans, also called coneflowers (not to be confused with purple coneflower), offer dazzling daisy-type flowers in flaming autumn colors from summer to fall. Native to North America, they reach 2–4 ft. with masses of flowers over a long period. Use these plants as accents, for cut flowers, for late bloom in borders or massed for color. *R. fulgida* var. *sullivantii* 'Goldsturm' has yellow petals with a black center. It grows to about 2 ft. with 3 in. flowers. For a background plant try 6 ft. *R. laciniata*. All are easy to grow in sun with average water and soil conditions. Zones 3–9.

Blanket flower

Gaillardia x grandiflora

Blanket flowers offer flashy daisy-like 4 in. blossoms that echo the warmth of summer and glow of autumn. Orange, bronze, maroon or red flowers often have tips of gold or yellow and are borne in great numbers on compact plants. Blanket flowers have a particularly long bloom time, from early summer into fall. Use gaillardias in masses or as accent plants, along border edges, in containers or as cut flowers. Plant in full sun, with average water and well-drained soil. If original crowns die out, divide and transplant newer perimeter shoots. Zones 3–10.

Candytuft

Iberis sempervirens

Dense, spreading mats covered with 2 in. clusters of tiny white flowers in spring make the candytuft a useful perennial along borders or in rock gardens and containers. This heirloom plant blooms all spring, yet the fine, glossy, dark green foliage looks good all year. Plants reach 8 in. high and spread to 2 ft., although 'Little Gem' is smaller. 'Snowflake' spreads more and offers larger flowers and foliage. Candytuft takes full sun and prefers a rich, well-drained soil. To keep plants compact, cut them back after they bloom. New plants can be grown from cuttings taken in summer. Zones 3–10.

Butterfly weed

Asclepias tuberosa

Clusters of bright orange flowers irresistible to butterflies make this perennial a star in the summer garden. Butterfly weed is very well behaved and easy. It never needs division and thrives in hot sun and in poor soils as long as they are well drained. The plant starts slowly from dormant roots late in spring but soon reaches about 3 ft. at bloom time. Use this perennial individually, massed and in dry and natural gardens. It withstands drought but generally does better when watered regularly. Zones 3–9.

Cardinal flower

Lobelia cardinalis

Cardinal flower, a native of the eastern United States, is known for brilliant red flowers on tall spikes. It grows wild in damp meadows and along streams; in the garden it prefers damp conditions in sun or part shade. The foliage forms small clumps from which 3–4 ft. spikes of 2 in. tubular flowers rise in the summer. As a striking accent, the cardinal flower can be used in shade or heirloom gardens or at the back of a bed. It also attracts hummingbirds and makes a nice cut flower. Divide every year or two after flowering. Zones 2–10.

Balloon flower
Platycodon grandiflorus

Swollen, round, balloon-like buds give way to bright star-shaped flowers on this plant. The 2 in. summer flowers are white, purple, blue and violet-blue; darker shades show accented veins. Plants reach 2 ft. in height with oval, medium green 3 in. leaves. 'Apoyama' is a 10 in. variety. Use balloon flowers for cool accents and massed in beds and borders. Plants prefer partial to full shade in warm climates but tolerate full sun in cool regions. Give them average, well-drained soil and regular watering.
Zones 3–9.

Cinquefoil
Potentilla species

Cinquefoils are neat spreading plants known for spring and summer flowers that resemble those of strawberry, but in warm colors. Some species are actually shrubs. Strawberry cinquefoil, *P. fragiformis*, has fuzzy, three-part leaves and bright yellow 1–2 in. flowers on a compact 5–8 in. plant. Tiny *P. x tonguei*, just 3 in. tall, has apricot flowers with maroon centers. Larger *P. nepalensis* 'Willmottiae' reaches 1 ft. with rose-colored flowers. Give cinquefoils sun to part shade, average water and well-drained soil and they'll perform well in your rock garden or along the front of the border.
Zones 4–10.

Christmas rose
Helleborus niger

Unusual greenish white flowers that bloom from December to March make the Christmas rose an interesting addition to the perennial bed. Plants reach 1 ft. with bold evergreen leaves that form neat mounds; individual leaf stalks rise from the ground even in harsh winter. Given a sheltered spot, the Christmas rose and its cousin the Lenten rose (*H. orientalis*) offer color when little else is showing. Use as border, accent or cut flower and in shade gardens. Hellebores like average, well-drained soil and part to full shade.
Zones 3–10.

Columbine

Aquilegia species

No perennial exemplifies grace and loveliness more than columbine. The spring flowers have short, broad inner petals above larger colorful spurs that bend down and backwards in a star pattern. Dwarf columbines are suited to rock gardens (*A. flabellata* 'Nana Alba' reaches just 6 in.) and larger 2 ft. plants are perfect for massing in groups, naturalizing in informal settings or including in shade, heirloom and cutting gardens. Give columbines good drainage, light shade to sun, and regular watering; deadhead for longer flowering. They're easy to grow from seed. Zones 3–10.

Coralbells

Heuchera species

Small mounds of foliage with airy stalks of white, pink or red flowers have made coralbells a welcome addition to perennial gardens for years. Up close, you can see the tiny bell-shaped flowers that provide a striking display of color lasting from spring into summer. Bressingham Hybrids come in red, pink, cream, green and white. The nearly round leaves are attractive too, turning from glossy green to an autumn bronze. These small plants work well in beds, rock gardens and massed in edgings. They like sun to part shade, average soil and regular watering. Zones 3–10.

Coreopsis

Coreopsis species

Also known as tickseed, coreopsis are popular because of their prolific, bright yellow blossoms in summer. Clumps of *C. grandiflora* grow to about 2 ft. high, sending up double flowers on 2 ft. stems. 'Early Sunrise' flowers early, before other coreopsis. *C. auriculata* 'Nana' is only 6 in. tall, perfect for rock gardens and border edges. Coreopsis are useful in a natural garden, as cut or heirloom flowers, and in the border. Plants are easy to grow from seed, often self-sowing. They take full sun, average to poor but well-drained soil, and regular watering. Zones 4–10.

Daylily

Hemerocallis species and hybrids

Each daylily flower is just what the name suggests, beautiful for a day. The striking colors and dazzling display make them worthy of just about any garden. Blooming in summer, daylilies can reach 1–4 ft. tall. The heirloom *H. fulva,* known as orange or tawny daylily, was the forerunner of today's hybrids that are available in red, pink, yellow, orange, lavender, purple and bicolors. Considered by some to be the easiest perennial to grow, daylilies are useful in beds, around foundations, in containers, as cut flowers and, for small varieties, in rock gardens. Daylilies are tolerant of most soils, adaptable to moist or dry conditions and take sun to partial shade. Zones 3–10.

Bleeding-heart
Dicentra species

These perennials with neat rows of heart-shaped flowers dangling like lockets above soft emerald foliage are elegant and lovely. Flowers come in pink, red and white in spring and summer. Use in shade and rock gardens, borders, heirloom plantings and for cut flowers. Common bleeding-heart, a native of Japan, is *D. spectabilis*. This old favorite reaches 2–3 ft. with 1 in. rose pink flowers and deeply lobed leaves. Fringed bleeding-heart, *D. eximia*, has finely cut blue-gray foliage mounding to 18 in. Give filtered light or partial shade, regular watering and a rich, well-drained soil. Zones 3–10.

Evening primrose
Oenothera species

Evening primroses provide masses of summer color with delicate-looking but long-lasting cupped flowers in pink, yellow and white. Plants have a tendency to spread, sending up new stems all around. *O. missourensis*, or Ozark sundrop, has 9 in.-high stems and large, 3–5 in. yellow flowers that open in the evening, making it perfect for a moonlight garden, rock garden or border edge. Mexican evening primrose, *O. berlandieri*, produces multitudes of pink flowers on 12–18 in. plants. It is invasive but works well on dry slopes or where it can spread naturally. Zones 5–10.

Gaura
Gaura lindheimer

For a tall, willowy garden accent, try gaura. This perennial produces tall flower spikes with pink buds that open to delicate white 1 in. blossoms from late spring through summer into fall. Gaura grows to 4 ft. with narrow dark green leaves. Overall, the effect is a light, airy plant. Use it at the back of borders, in low-maintenance gardens and in drought-tolerant plantings. Gaura takes heat and needs only moderate watering and a light, well-drained loamy soil. It's easily grown from seed and self-sows. Zones 6–10.

Gazania

Gazania hybrids

The low-growing gazania, a star performer in the spring and summer garden, offers floral carpets in maroon, red, pink, bronze, white, cream and yellow. Daisy-like flowers range 2–4 in.; many have dark centers radiating to yellow or orange. Plants either form tight 10 in.–wide clumps of oblong, dark green leaves or trail with creeping stems and gray leaves. Clumping gazanias are valuable in rock gardens, along border edges or massed near lawns and walkways. Trailing varieties spread rapidly; they can be used as ground covers, on banks or in containers or window boxes. Zones 8–10.

Hollyhock

Alcea rosea

Height and splendor are what hollyhocks bring to the perennial garden. Tall stalks of numerous cupped flowers in red, pink, yellow, white and mixed colors bloom in summer. Single and double flowers are available as are larger varieties. Plants reach 6–8 ft. and may need staking if not supported by a wall or fence. Use these formidable heirloom perennials as background plants or in the center of island perennial gardens. Hollyhocks like full sun and a rich deep soil for the roots to penetrate. They are short-lived and should be replanted every 2 years for the best performance. Zones 2–10.

Goldenrod

Solidago hybrids

The goldenrod's arching plume of soft yellow in summer and fall lends a sunny warmth to the perennial garden. Plants are 2–3 ft. tall, with slender stems of long, tapering foliage. They have a tenacious quality, growing wild along roadsides in the Midwest and eastern regions. In the garden, the hybrids are less invasive. They serve as welcome late color in borders, natural gardens, drought-tolerant plantings and in spots where soil is marginal. 'Goldenmosa' is a good bright yellow, blooming earlier than most. Plant in full sun to part shade. Propagate by division every 3 years in spring. Zones 3–10.

Lamb's-ears

Stachys byzantina

A longtime garden standout that tempts you to touch, lamb's-ears combines appealing gray foliage with a texture true to its name. Foliage is the attraction and the velvety, silver 6 in. leaves have the shape as well as the feel of a lamb's ear. Plants form 10 in. clumps perfect as a small-space ground cover or for interest in beds, borders, heirloom plantings and large rock gardens. Reddish purple flowers appear in summer and fall, but are not showy. Lamb's-ears is easy to grow and tolerant of sun or part shade, good to poor soil and moderate watering. Zones 4–10.

Gay-feather

Liatris species

Gay-feather's striking flower spikes in purple, lavender, and white make a bold statement in any perennial garden. Clumps of grassy foliage give way to brilliant spikes ranging 2–5 ft. Flowers open from the top downward, an oddity in the plant world. Also called button snakeroot or blazing star, these perennials bloom in summer and early fall. Use them as accents at the back of the border or massed in large beds. Gay-feathers are easy to grow in sunny spots with average but well-drained soil. They prefer regular watering but tolerate drought conditions if given occasional deep watering. Zones 3–10.

Lavender

Lavandula species

Lavender is on the fringes as a perennial, since it is often classified as a shrub. But it offers such aromatic summer beauty it's definitely worthy of consideration. The gray-green foliage contrasts strikingly with purple to lavender flowers in spring, summer and (in mild climates) fall. Use in perennial or herb borders, rock gardens, as small hedges or along walks. French lavender grows 3 ft. tall with flowers on short spikes. English lavender is the classic choice, reaching 4 ft.; Spanish lavender with its showier flowers is only 2 ft. All like sun, well-drained soil and little water. Zones 7–10.

Delphinium

Delphinium species

The majestic delphinium has brought gardeners satisfaction and joy since the seventeenth century. Known for pure blue flowers, perennial delphiniums also come in rich purples, raspberry, white, pink, lavender, yellow and multicolored varieties. Flowers form on 5–7 ft. spikes; new hybrids have compact 2–3 ft. spikes that require less staking. Soft green leaves are maple-like. For height in the border, for cut flowers or for background plantings, delphiniums offer elegant form during the summer. Give them protection from hot summer sun and drying winds, rich, well-drained soil and support for flower stalks. Zones 3–10.

Lilyturf

Liriope muscari or *spicata*

This grass-like perennial forms tight clumps of dark green or variegated foliage sometimes accented with gold or cream stripes. *L. muscari* is versatile, taking part to full shade. It blooms in summer, sending up spikes of tiny lavender flowers on 15 in. stems. *L. spicata* is slightly shorter and hardier. Use it in colder climates, cutting it to the ground in spring. Use either species wherever you want grassy tufts—along a border, in a rock garden or in the shade. Both like regular watering, filtered sun or shade and well-drained soil. Zones 5–10 (*L. muscari*) and 4–10 (*L. spicata*).

Martha Washington geranium

Pelargonium x domesticum

Also called Lady Washington geranium, this plant offers impressive 2 in. flowers in showy two-tone combinations with brilliant centers. Clusters come in white, pink, red, lavender, purple and rose. Plants bloom in spring and summer and have heart-shaped, deep green leaves. Plants reach 3 ft. both in height and spread. Use as accents in the border or in containers and hanging baskets. Plant in full sun or light shade. These perennials prefer average watering—once a week in warm weather—and well-drained soil. Cut back or pinch to keep the plant from becoming woody. Cuttings root easily. Zone 10.

Maltese-cross

Lychnis chalcedonica

The Maltese-cross has dense clusters of brilliant scarlet, cross-shaped 2 in. flowers. The rounded 4 in. flower heads rise above upward-pointing, lance-shaped leaves on 2–3 ft. plants. Also known as Jerusalem-cross, this summer-bloomer dates back to the seventeenth century when it was planted in settlers' gardens. Use as an accent, in combination with other warm colors, among evergreens or in heirloom plantings. 'Alba' provides white flowers. Give the Maltese-cross full sun to light shade, average, well-drained soil and regular watering. Zones 3–10.

Obedient plant

Physostegia virginiana

Well behaved because flowers can be twisted into desired positions, and valuable for late summer color, the obedient plant is a unique addition to the perennial garden. Spreading clumps of 5 in. toothed leaves send up tapering 3 ft. flower spikes in purple, pink and white. Flowers are arranged in neat, dense rows and bloom into autumn. Use this perennial as a focal point, in small masses, in natural areas where it can spread and in cutting gardens. The obedient plant takes sun to partial shade, regular watering and average soil. Divide every 1–2 years to keep plants neat and compact. Zones 3–10.

PERENNIAL GALLERY

Japanese anemone
Anemone x hybrida

Bringing beauty to the fall garden, Japanese anemones provide airy sprays of 2 in. flowers on slender stems. Flower stalks reach 4 ft., rising above clumps of deep green maple-like leaves. Flower color ranges from white to pink in single or double blossoms. Despite a delicate look, plants are easy to grow and tolerate cold and neglect when established. Give the plants rich, well-drained soil and partial to full sun. Mulch clumps in winter in cold climates. Use in partial shade or woodland settings; mass in beds and borders. Zones 5–10.

Phlox
Phlox species

Intense color and varying growth styles make these indigenous North American perennials excellent choices for the home garden. Phlox bloom from spring into autumn in lots of colors—red, pink, white, blue, apricot, purple and rose. Flowers consist of clusters or single star-shaped blossoms. *P. paniculata* and *P. carolina* are popular heirloom choices, with summer flowers on 3–4 ft. stems. *P. subulata* is perfect for rock gardens, forming a dense mat of solid color in early spring. Use as massed color, tall background plants and small border specimens. Give phlox full sun to part shade and deep, rich, well-drained soil. Tall varieties may need staking. Zones 3–9.

Peony
Paeonia lactiflora

It's no wonder peonies have been perennial garden favorites for hundreds of years. They combine sensational flowers with large, deeply veined, dark green foliage that is attractive all season. Hundreds of cultivars are available with 3–10 in. flowers in red, white, cream, pink and yellow. Spring flowers come in full double pompons, semi-double and single blossoms. Dense foliage clumps range 1–4 ft. wide. Peonies are beautiful as focal points or massed in beds where they have room to grow. Give peonies full sun and rich, well-drained soil. Zones 3–8.

Pincushion flower

Scabiosa caucasica

The pincushion flower, with stamens resembling tiny pins surrounded by colorful, soft, rounded petals, is valued for its unique form. Summer flowers are 2–3 in. and come in blue or white on slender 2 ft. stems. Foliage grows in clumps with deeply cut, slender, medium green leaves. Pincushions make fine cut flowers, work as border or rock garden plants and look lovely massed together. Give plants full sun, and average to sandy, well-drained soil with some organic content. Plants are easy to start from seed. Zones 3–10.

Plantain lily

Hosta species

Most perennials are valued for their flowers, but the plantain lily is prized for its bold, beautiful foliage. The foliage is quite varied: some leaves are wavy, some are edged in yellow or cream and some are blue-green. Hostas offer flowers too, with summer blooms in violet, lavender and white forming on tall spikes. Plants form mounds from a few inches to several feet in height and width. Use hostas in shade and rock gardens and to accent other plants in borders and beds. Give hostas partial to full shade, rich to average, well-drained soil and regular watering. Zones 3–9.

Pinks

Dianthus species

Pinks include a broad category of old-fashioned, fragrant border perennials with attractive gray-green foliage and summer flowers. Cottage pinks, *D. plumarius,* form small, dense 6 in. mounds with 10–12 in. stems topped by flowers in red, pink, white and bicolors. Carnations, *D. caryophyllus,* are classic choices for the fragrant garden. Maiden pinks, *D. deltoides,* form low mats with faintly fragrant flowers. Use pinks in borders, masses, rock gardens, containers and window boxes. These heirloom plants thrive in sunny spots with light, very well drained soil. Hot summer regions require some shade protection and a winter covering helps pinks in cold climates. Zones 3–10.

Primrose

Primula species

No plant quite captures the joy and delight of early spring as well as a primrose. You'll find countless choices under this broad category, including flowers of every color. *P.* x *polyantha* are the easiest to grow, with 8 in. stems supporting clusters of bright yellow-centered flowers. The Juliana hybrids are miniature versions, reaching only 4 in., with many appealing color combinations. Larger primroses that thrive in damp soil include the 2–3 ft. Candelabra group and the late-flowering Sikkimensis group. Give primulas partial shade, rich, moist soil and regular watering. Zones 3–10.

69

PERENNIAL GALLERY

Lupine

Lupinus Russell Hybrids

Lupines offer dramatic spires in the spring perennial garden. Plants form bushy clumps with dark green leaves resembling an open hand. Tall, pointed flower spikes come in many colors, including red, pink, blue, purple, yellow, orange, white, cream and bicolors. Some selections stay small, reaching only 1–2 ft., but most grow 4–5 ft. Use lupines in natural areas, in small groups or as accents (foliage and flower). Give lupines protection from drying sun in summer, well-drained soil rich with organic matter and plenty of water. They are generally short-lived and do best where summers are cool. Zones 4–9.

Red-hot-poker

Kniphofia species

Perfectly named, this perennial offers exotic beauty and warm interest with its vertical torches of tall flower spikes in red, orange, yellow, pink and cream. Tubular flowers at the bottom of the stem are lighter than those at the top. Some plants bloom in late spring, others in summer and fall. Kniphofias range 2–4 ft. tall, forming clumps of thick, coarse, grassy foliage that contrasts well with broad-leaved perennials. Use as a garden accent, for contrast, in large rock gardens or as cut flowers. All like full sun, rich, moist, well-drained soil and regular to moderate water. Zones 6–10.

Purple coneflower

Echinacea purpurea

Rich, daisy-like flowers with dark, mounded centers put the purple coneflower in a class of its own. Actually you'll find flowers in pink, red and white as well as purple. Blooming in summer, this perennial produces many 2–4 ft. flower stems and dense clumps of rough, oval, dark green foliage. Use these as individuals within a bed, grouped for mass color, in natural gardens and in cutting gardens. Give the purple coneflower full sun, rich, well-drained soil and moderate watering. Propagate by division and seeds. Zones 3–10.

Red valerian
Centranthus ruber

This easy-to-grow perennial presents bright, puffy clusters of tiny star-like flowers from spring through summer. Red, white and pink flowers are borne on stalks that rise above 3 ft.–high blue-green foliage. Also known as Jupiter's-beard, this plant is useful on banks, in dry and natural landscapes and massed in the background of beds and borders. Cut off the first blooms for a second flowering. It self-sows in mild climates. Give this plant sun to partial shade, average soil and moderate to little watering. Zones 5–10.

Sea pink
Armeria species

Sea pink's dense mounds of grassy foliage support a profusion of short stems with small, round flower clusters in pink, white, rose and red. The short, dark green foliage makes a neat clump that spreads a bit each year. Flower pompons appear on 6–10 in. stems in spring and continue year-round in mild regions. These easy perennials work wonderfully along border edges, in rock gardens, along walks, as ground cover in small spaces, as cut flowers and massed for a lovely, low splash of color. They take well-drained soil, full sun and moderate watering. Zones 3–10.

Sage
Salvia species

Cool blues, fragrant foliage and long flowering periods make the many sages perfect selections for perennial borders. Plants range from rock garden dwarfs to 5 ft. vertical accents. Summer and fall flowers are borne in great numbers on slender stalks in blue, white and purple. Foliage varies from purple on *S. officinalis* 'Purpurea' to gray-green on *S.* x *superba,* one of the most cold-tolerant sages. Use as focal points in rock gardens and borders, in natural gardens or in cutting gardens. Salvias are easy to grow, taking full sun, average to poor soil and moderate watering. Zones 5–10.

Shasta daisy
Chrysanthemum x *superbum*

This plant is a classic in the perennial border because of its large, white daisy flowers and glossy, dark green leaves. Plants are notably long-blooming, producing many gold-centered 2–6 in. flowers from June until frost. Cultivars now include single and double varieties. Plants range 2–3 ft. tall, forming hardy clumps. Use these traditional daisies in beds and borders, as cut flowers and in natural gardens. Shasta daisies like full sun to partial shade (in hot summer regions), rich, well-drained soil and regular watering. Divide in spring for new plants. Zones 4–10.

PERENNIAL GALLERY

Siberian iris
Iris sibirica

Iris has long been a garden favorite because of its many forms and colors. Siberian iris is especially prized for its easy nature, cold tolerance and colorful flowers. Early summer blossoms are medium sized for iris, and come in blue, white, pink, yellow, maroon, violet and rose. Long, slender sword-like leaves form clumps reaching 1–4 ft., depending on the cultivar. Use the Siberian iris as an accent among broad-leaf perennials, in groupings, in naturalized settings and for cut flowers. Plant rhizomes 1–2 in. deep in average, well-drained soil in areas with full sun to partial shade. Zones 4–10.

Stokes' aster
Stokesia laevis

Stokes' aster, with arresting 4 in. flowers, is an heirloom perennial admired for its long blooming time and adaptability. Blue, lavender, pink or white flowers resemble annual asters with deeply cut petals radiating from light-colored centers. In mild regions flowers are produced year round; in cooler regions expect blooms in summer and fall. Foliage forms short clumps to about 1 ft. tall with dark green, narrow leaves. Use this North American native, for cut flowers and among heirloom plantings. Give the plants full sun, average, well-drained soil and moderate watering. Zones 5–10.

Speedwell
Veronica species

Rising like colorful arrows from clumps of glossy, dark green foliage, the flower spikes of speedwell bring a cool grace to the perennial garden. In summer, tiny star-shaped flowers in purple, pink, blue or white form on tapered stalks. Plants grow as tall clumps 3–4 ft., as medium perennials in the 1–3 ft. range and as tiny 6 in. ground covers. Use tall species in background plantings, mid-sized massed or as accents, and creepers for rock gardens or to cascade over garden walls. Veronicas prefer sun or partial shade, average, well-drained soil and regular watering. Zones 3–10.

Stonecrop

Sedum species

The fleshy, thick leaves and striking flowers of stonecrop come in a variety of sizes; growth habits range from low creepers to 1–2 ft.–wide clumps of many individual stalks. Flowers come in pink, red, purple, yellow and white and form on dense clusters of individual star-shaped florets. These perennials are very easy to grow and produce flowers from May to October. Use stonecrops in dry, sunny locations, in rock gardens, for contrast in borders and beds and in containers. Stonecrops prefer full sun, well-drained, sandy soil and moderate watering. Zones 3–10.

Wormwood

Artemisia species

Valued for its foliage, wormwood provides striking contrast with leaves that range through the grays and gray-greens to almost white. Plants range from compact mounds just inches high to shrubby 2–4 ft. specimens. Besides interesting color, leaves have a nice variety of shapes and textures. *A. schmidtiana* has delicate, feathery foliage and *A. ludoviciana* sports narrow silvery leaves. For effective contrast in color and texture, try wormwoods along borders, in rock gardens and among naturalized plantings. Wormwoods prefer full sun, average to poor but well-drained soil and moderate watering. Zones 4–10.

Transvaal daisy

Gerbera jamesonii

Exquisite, refined and substantial describe the Transvaal or gerbera daisy. With each perfectly shaped petal, gerberas raise daisies to another level. Flowers are 4–5 in. with rings of petals and light green centers. Colors include red, yellow, pink and cream. You'll find the 7–18 in. flower stems supporting blossoms from summer into autumn, especially in mild regions. Clumps of dark green, lobed leaves reach about 1 ft. Use as excellent container or window-box plants, in beds and borders, in masses or as individuals. Transvaal daisies need sun, well-drained, highly organic soil, regular fertilizer and moderate watering. Watch for snails. Zones 8–10.

Yarrow

Achillea species

Yarrows have been perennial garden favorites since the 1800s. Their appeal is in their dependable service, long flowering periods and versatility. Plants produce flat clusters of yellow, white, red, pink and cream flowers in spring and summer or year-round in mild climates. Clumps of finely divided, lacy leaves grow 6 in.–3 ft. on tough plants able to tolerate neglect. Yarrows are valuable in beds and borders, rock gardens, dry plantings, cutting gardens, massed groupings or for foliage accents. Yarrows take full sun, tolerate poor soil and are drought tolerant. Zones 2–10.

73

PERENNIAL GRASSES

For a change of pace, include ornamental grasses in your perennial garden. Their colorful foliage harmonizes and contrasts with flowering perennials to create splendid results. Their adaptability makes them useful in sun or shade, in large areas or rock gardens and in rich or poor soil.

Blue oat grass
Helictotrichon sempervirens

Blue oat grass displays bright blue-gray, very narrow leaves on clumps that reach 2–3 ft. Foliage is rather stiff, but beautifully colored—much like a large version of blue fescue. Tan flower plumes rise just above the foliage in summer. Use this grass for graceful accents and contrast in beds and borders, in dry gardens or in natural settings, especially near rocks. Blue oat grass prefers sun and takes average to good soil as long as it has adequate drainage. Give moderate watering. The best time to plant or divide is early spring. Zones 5–10.

Eulalia grass
Miscanthus sinensis

Eulalia grass is not for small spaces. Its graceful foliage reaches 5–6 ft. as it forms large clumps with blue-green, finely toothed leaves. 'Zebrinus' has yellow bands running across the leaves; 'Variegatus' has leaves accented lengthwise with white stripes. 'Gracillimus', the maiden grass, is more delicate and slightly shorter. Use these perennial grasses as accents, near water, as windbreaks or as a background planting. All produce tan flower panicles suitable for dried arrangements. They take full sun, are very hardy, tolerate just about any soil that drains and like moderate to heavy watering. Cut back in winter. Zones 5–10.

Giant feather grass
Stipa gigantea

Great stems of oat-like yellow flowers towering 6 ft. over clumps of arching, narrow leaves on the giant feather grass create a soft, windswept look in the perennial garden. The narrow green leaves reach 2–3 ft. Tall flower stalks have clusters of tiny purplish flowers that turn yellow as they mature in mid summer. Use the giant feather grass for bold accents in spacious gardens, along garden boundaries and for contrast. It takes full sun, good soil and regular watering until established, when it tolerates some drought. Zones 7–10.

Fescue

Festuca species

Fescues are attractive grasses that form tight tufts with soft, thread-like foliage in colors from steely blue-gray to blue green. Blue fescue, *F. ovina* 'glauca', is a small variety reaching 4–10 in., making it ideal for rock gardens, ground covers, or bed and border accents. *F. amethystina* is larger—up to 18 in.—and more green in color. All fescues like sun to partial shade, moderate watering in hot summer regions and well-drained soil. Clumps should be divided in spring if crowded or when the centers begin to die out. Zones 4–10.

Japanese blood grass

Imperata cylindrica 'Rubra'

This perennial grass lends a striking accent to the garden with its slender, upright, dark red leaves. Many consider this to be the most colorful ornamental grass. Clumps reach 1–2 ft. tall with colorful leaves from spring to autumn. Plants die to the ground in winter. Use as colorful accents, in rock gardens and in sunny beds and borders. Clumps spread slowly so plant close together. Japanese blood grass takes full sun, average to good soil and moderate watering. Zones 7–10.

Fountain grass

Pennisetum species

True to their name, fountain grasses offer arching, willowy clumps of narrow leaves. Plants reach 2–3 ft. in both height and spread. Fountain grass produces thick plumes with pink, tan, copper, bronze and purple hues in summer and fall. Chinese pennisetum, *P. alopecuroides,* is a hardy grass that reaches 3 ft. and sports pinkish tan flowers. The tender *P. setaceum* forms 2 ft.–wide mounds with coppery or purplish flowering stems. Use these grasses for accent or contrast and as individual specimens. They take full sun, average to rich soil and moderate watering. Zones 6–10.

Sedge

Carex species

Though not true grasses, sedges have a definite grass-like appearance with arching, erect, narrow leaves. Fox red curly sedge, *C. buchananii,* is an attractive 2–3 ft. plant with reddish bronze leaves that are curled on the ends. *C. morrowii* 'expallida', or variegated Japanese sedge, makes a compact 1 ft. mound with green leaves striped in white. Use sedges for focal points, near ponds or streams, in rock gardens, along bed edges, in containers or in wet places. They take full sun to light shade and regular to very damp soil. Zones 5–10.

PLANTING ZONE MAP

HOW TO USE THIS MAP

The map outlines eleven zones in North America for the purpose of determining plant hardiness. It is based on the United States Department of Agriculture's figures for minimum winter temperatures.

It's important to understand that the zones are designed to provide basic information, not absolute parameters.

You may, for example, live very near a zone border or in a microclimate such as a sunny, south-facing valley. If that's the case, you may have slightly higher temperatures more like those in the next warmer zone. Or perhaps you're near the highest elevation of your region in a windy spot with temperatures more like the next cooler zone.

Good winter protection will extend the life of your perennials in marginal zones where plants may be in danger during the coldest months. Use a protective layer of mulch—such as leaves, evergreen boughs or straw—over the plants. The colder it is or the less hardy the plant, the more mulch you need. Use a foot or more if you're in zone 3 or cooler or are in the coldest recommended zone for a particular plant. Fall mulching helps keep crowns from freezing and thawing repeatedly.

On the other hand, you may live where heat is the source of potential damage to your perennials. Shade from arbors or trees will help keep afternoon sun from damaging plants. Regular watering and a moisture-saving layer of mulch on the soil also help.

Watching and working with nature is part of the excitement and challenge gardening offers. Whether it's adapting to nature's sometimes harsh conditions or reveling in the beauty of a single flower, true satisfaction comes from the ongoing process of making the garden the best it can be.

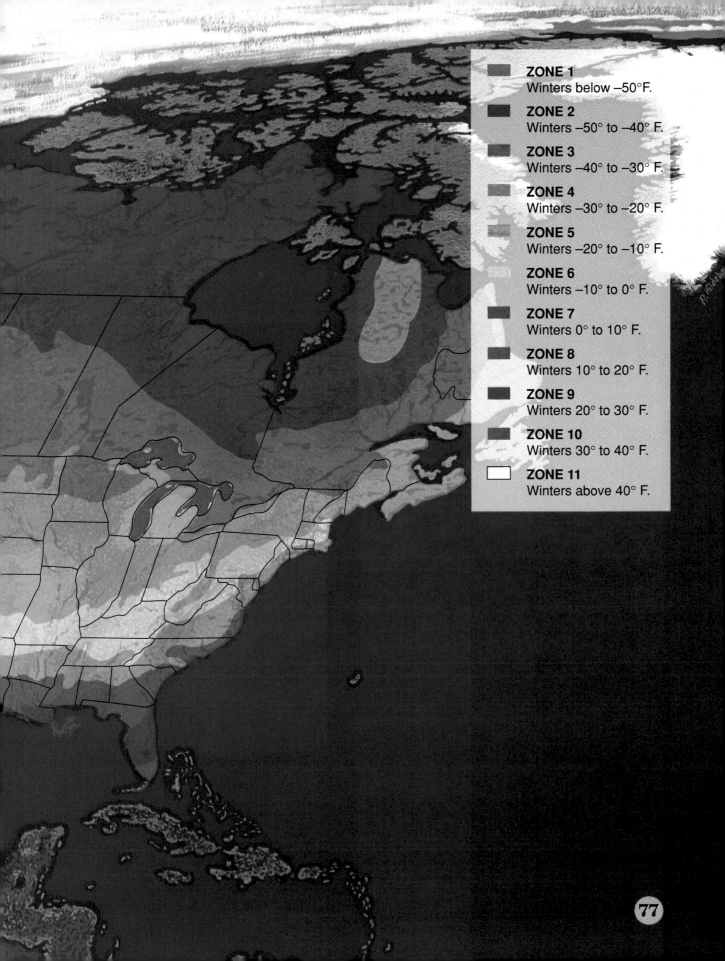

ZONE 1
Winters below −50°F.

ZONE 2
Winters −50° to −40° F.

ZONE 3
Winters −40° to −30° F.

ZONE 4
Winters −30° to −20° F.

ZONE 5
Winters −20° to −10° F.

ZONE 6
Winters −10° to 0° F.

ZONE 7
Winters 0° to 10° F.

ZONE 8
Winters 10° to 20° F.

ZONE 9
Winters 20° to 30° F.

ZONE 10
Winters 30° to 40° F.

ZONE 11
Winters above 40° F.

INDEX

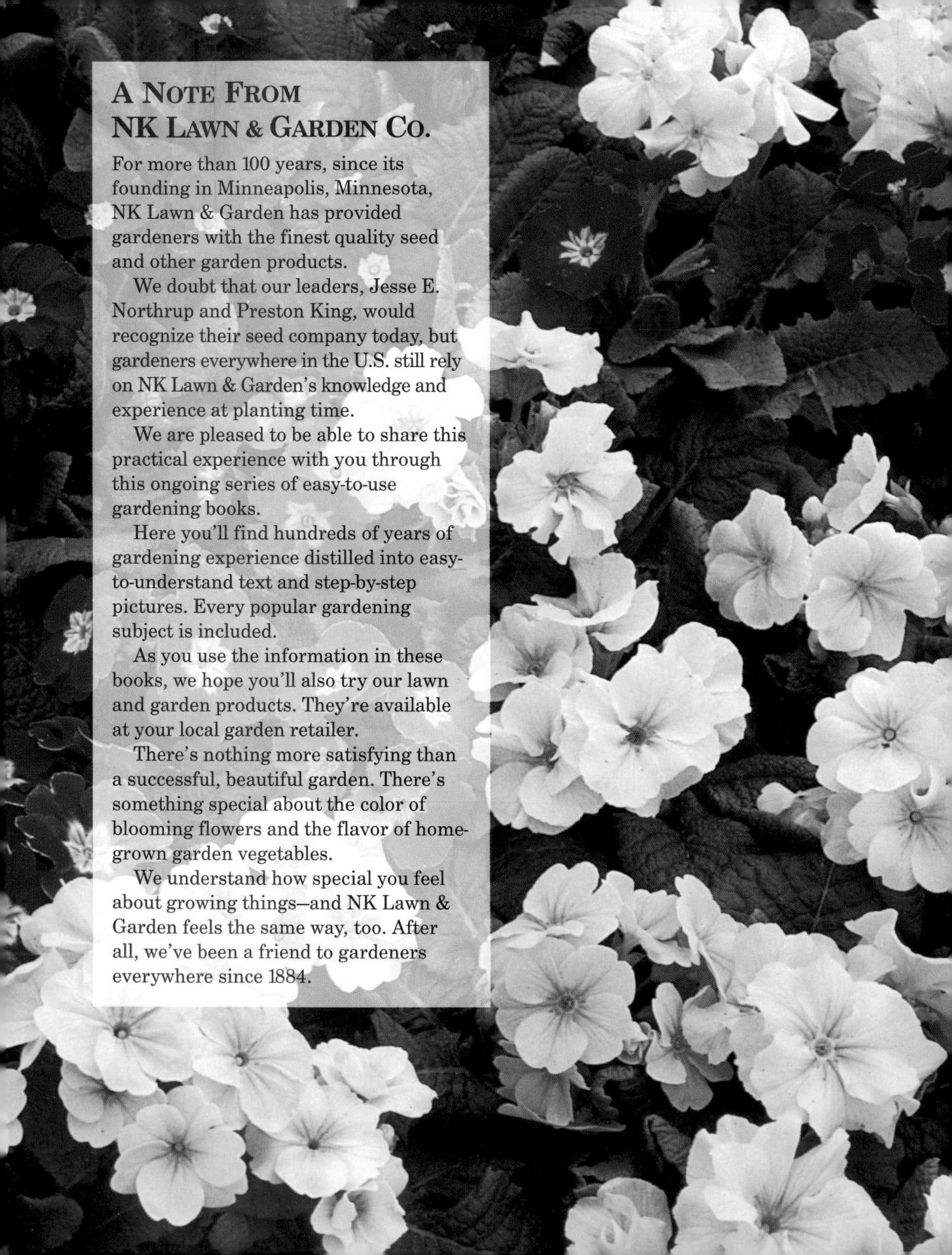

A NOTE FROM NK LAWN & GARDEN CO.

For more than 100 years, since its founding in Minneapolis, Minnesota, NK Lawn & Garden has provided gardeners with the finest quality seed and other garden products.

We doubt that our leaders, Jesse E. Northrup and Preston King, would recognize their seed company today, but gardeners everywhere in the U.S. still rely on NK Lawn & Garden's knowledge and experience at planting time.

We are pleased to be able to share this practical experience with you through this ongoing series of easy-to-use gardening books.

Here you'll find hundreds of years of gardening experience distilled into easy-to-understand text and step-by-step pictures. Every popular gardening subject is included.

As you use the information in these books, we hope you'll also try our lawn and garden products. They're available at your local garden retailer.

There's nothing more satisfying than a successful, beautiful garden. There's something special about the color of blooming flowers and the flavor of home-grown garden vegetables.

We understand how special you feel about growing things—and NK Lawn & Garden feels the same way, too. After all, we've been a friend to gardeners everywhere since 1884.